T0358422

Routledge Revivals

Efficiency, Equality and the Ownership of Property

First published in 1964, this is a study of the extreme inequalities in the ownership of property, in economies across the globe. Professor Meade examines in depth the economic, demographic and social factors which lead to such inequalities. He considers a wide range of remedial policies – educational development, reformed death duties and capital taxes, demographic policies, trade union action, the socialization of property, the development of a property-owning democracy, the expansion of the welfare state.

The argument is expressed in precise analytical terms, but the main exposition is free of mathematics and technical jargon and is designed for the interested layman as well as the economist.

Efficiency, Equality and the Ownership of Property

J. E. Meade

Routledge
Taylor & Francis Group

First published in 1964
by George Allen & Unwin Ltd

This edition first published in 2012 by Routledge
2 Park Square, Milton Park, Abingdon, Oxon, OX14 4RN

Simultaneously published in the USA and Canada
by Routledge
711 Third Avenue, New York, NY 10017

Routledge is an imprint of the Taylor & Francis Group, an informa business

Publisher's Note
The publisher has gone to great lengths to ensure the quality of this reprint but
points out that some imperfections in the original copies may be apparent.

Disclaimer
The publisher has made every effort to trace copyright holders and welcomes
correspondence from those they have been unable to contact.

A Library of Congress record exists under ISBN: 65009733

ISBN 13: 978-0-415-52626-5 (hbk)
ISBN 13: 978-0-203-10662-4 (ebk)

EFFICIENCY, EQUALITY
AND
THE OWNERSHIP OF
PROPERTY

BY

J. E. MEADE
C.B., F.B.A.

London
GEORGE ALLEN & UNWIN LTD
RUSKIN HOUSE MUSEUM STREET

FIRST PUBLISHED IN 1964
SECOND IMPRESSION 1969

SBN 04 330151 7

PRINTED IN GREAT BRITAIN
BY PHOTOLITHOGRAPHY
UNWIN BROTHERS LIMITED
WOKING AND LONDON

PREFACE

This short book is based on lectures given to students of the University and of the Business School in Stockholm in May 1964. I would like to thank these two institutions for the invitation to lecture and the British Council and the Council of Europe for making my visit possible. I would like also to thank the editor of the *Economic Journal* for permission to incorporate certain passages from my article 'Mauritius: a Case Study in Malthusian Economics' published in the *Economic Journal, September* 1961. The arguments in Chapter V of this book have been much influenced by a thesis (alas, still unpublished) by Mr. D. G. Champernowne on the causes of economic inequalities. I am also much indebted to my wife for suggesting a number of improvements in my exposition.

The subject matter of these lectures is of great and (with the development of automation) of growing importance; but it is strangely neglected—particularly in the United Kingdom. In Sweden there is (i) a progressive tax on capital gains, (ii) a progressive annual tax on total personal wealth, (iii) a progressive tax on gifts *inter vivos*, and (iv) a progressive tax on individual bequests. I implore any of my fellow countrymen who read this book not to object: 'It can't be done.'

J.E.M.

Christ's College, Cambridge
May 1964

CONTENTS

PREFACE 7

I *Economic Efficiency and Distributional Justice* 11

II *The Present Position in the Developed Countries* 27

III *The Trade Union State* 35

IV *The Welfare State* 38

V *A Property-Owning Democracy* 40

VI *A Socialist State* 66

VII *Conclusion* 75

Appendix I. The Distribution of Personal Incomes. The United Kingdom, 1959 78

Appendix II. The Accumulation of Personal Property 82

Appendix III. A Proposed Scale for a new Legacy and Gift Duty 88

Index 91

LIST OF TABLES

1. Distribution of Personal Wealth in the United Kingdom   27

2. Distribution of Personal Incomes from Property and Earnings, United Kingdom, 1959   29

3. The Stock of Tangible and Intangible Capital in the United States, 1929 and 1957   31

4. Mean I.Q.s of Parents and Child According to Class of Parents   50

5. Personal Incomes (before deduction of tax) in the United Kingdom, 1959   79

6. Personal Incomes and the Net National Income Compared   80–81

7. A Proposed Scale for a Revised Duty on Gifts and Legacies   89

I

Economic Efficiency and Distributional Justice

The following pages are an exercise in the analysis of the dual function of the price mechanism. The price of a commodity or of a factor of production is a determinant both of the use which will be made of that commodity or factor of production and of the real income which the owner of the commodity or factor of production will receive as a result of its sale. These we will call the 'efficiency' and the 'distributional' aspects of the price. As is well known to all professional economists, relative prices properly used either in a competitive market or else by a planning authority can help to guide the economic system to an 'efficient' use of resources, that is to say, to a state of affairs in which resources are so used that it would be impossible to make one citizen better off without making any other worse off. For if a high price is charged for scarce resources and a low price for plentiful resources, their users will always try to satisfy their needs in 'efficient' ways which use relatively little of the scarce resources and relatively much of the plentiful resources; and this will be true whether the users be entrepreneurs buying materials and other factors of production as inputs into some productive process or whether they be housewives buying consumption goods and services. But such an 'efficient' system may, of course, lead to a very undesirable distribution of real wealth. If citizen A owns nothing except a factor (e.g. his own unskilled labour) whose price is low and needs for his family's welfare goods whose price is high, he will be very poor, as compared with citizen B who happens to own a factor (e.g. a scarce natural resource) whose price is high and who happens to need for his family's enjoyment goods which are very cheap.

11

It is not, of course, my contention that a policy of *laissez faire*, leaving everything to be determined by the free play of market forces, would alone lead to a fully efficient use of resources. Professional economists are well aware of the obstacles to such a solution which must be overcome by various acts of governmental policy.

(i) Total effective demand for goods and services must be controlled by monetary and budgetary policy to maintain full employment and a background for economic growth.

(ii) Forecasting and planning *à la française* or in the mode of the United Kingdom's National Economic Development Council is necessary so that the many independent decision-making units may have a better and more consistent set of views about what future conditions will be like.

(iii) Monopolistic powers and market imperfections will cause discrepancies between prices and costs. Legislation against restrictive practices, control of prices, greater freedom for the import of competing products are among the measures which may be appropriate to deal with some of these problems. In other cases socialization and central public management may be the appropriate remedy.

(iv) There are innumerable cases of external economies and diseconomies (such as the congestion, noise, and stench of motor traffic in our cities) where government taxes and subsidies or other regulations are needed to bring private and social interests into harmony. In many cases such as police, defence, and justice the social concern is so predominant over the private interest that the activity is best conducted directly by the public authority.

(v) Consumers are ignorant and gullible. It is, therefore, desirable for the State to discourage private commercial advertisement and to foster disinterested consumer research and information services.

And so one could go on. But these are matters with which it is not my intention to deal on the present occasion. My present point is simply that even when the State is doing all that it should to make the system work efficiently, it will still be necessary to use the price mechanism as a guide to efficiency. In a modern complex economy the State must set the background of institutions and policies which will enable the system to harmonize social and private interests; but it is still necessary to attach price tags to the various factors of production and to the various final goods and services in order to guide those who have the day-to-day decisions to make (whether these be private entrepreneurs, the servants of public authorities, or individual housewives) as to what is plentiful and what is scarce. But prices used for this efficiency purpose may result in a very undesirable distribution of income and wealth.

There are many instances of this dilemma. A good example is the international market for primary products. It may often happen that a low price of a plentiful primary product is needed on world efficiency grounds to make the fullest use of this plentiful resource, but the producers of the primary product may be among the poorest citizens of the world. In a paper on 'International Commodity Policy'[1] I have tried to devise a policy which would divorce the 'efficiency' from the 'distributional' effects of the prices of primary products.

In these pages I am going to attempt the same task in a rather more elaborate manner for another and perhaps even more basic price. The price with which I shall be concerned is the wage rate of labour, the level of which can have most important 'efficiency' and 'distributional' effects. The policy measures and institutional reforms with which I shall primarily be concerned are those which influence the ownership of property. Such reforms have recently been strangely neglected by economists and politicians; but it will be my purpose to suggest that they might offer in the long run the principal means for reconciling the desired 'efficiency' and 'distributional' aspects of the level of the real wage rate.

The dilemma in the case of the real wage rate presents itself at present in its starkest form in some of the over-

[1] The paper was written for the United Nations Conference on Trade and Development. It is reproduced in *Lloyds Bank Review*, July 1964.

populated underdeveloped countries of the world. In an article published in 1961[1] I have already tried to outline the nature of this price dilemma in the case of one such economy—that of Mauritius, which can be taken as a microcosm typical of the many and large underdeveloped countries of the world in which there is a population explosion.

Mauritius is a small sugar-producing island in the Indian Ocean with a high and very rapidly increasing population. It is the outstanding example of a monocrop economy with 99 per cent of its exports and 40 to 50 per cent of its national output consisting of sugar. The big sugar factories and the greater part of the best land are owned by rich estate owners, mainly persons of French origin. The sugar estates are worked by comparatively poor workers mainly of Indian origin. In 1946–47 malaria was eliminated. The death rate fell from about 44 to 14 per thousand and the birth rate did not fall. The population began to grow at 3 per cent per annum. Since all those who will be of working age in fifteen years time have already been born, it is possible to calculate that, whatever may now happen to the birth rate, the working force in 15 years time will be 50 per cent greater than it is now. Thus the pressure of population upon resources which is already great is bound to become much more intense in the future.

Let us consider what classical economic analysis would have to say on this issue. Mauritius will be an economy in which unskilled labour is extremely plentiful and land and capital equipment are scarce. Such a situation would be one in which, in the classical competitive economy, the rent of land and the rates of profit and interest would rise and the real wage-rate would fall. This would give every incentive to private producers as well as to public authorities to go in for the production of things which required much labour and relatively little land and capital for their production and, in the production of any product or service, to choose those processes and techniques of production which used much labour and little land and capital.

[1] 'Mauritius: a Case Study in Malthusian Economics', *Economic Journal*, September 1961. The following paragraphs are based on this article.

The ultimate purpose is, of course, not to give employment, but to obtain the largest possible output from the community's (scarce) resources of land and capital and (plentiful) resources of labour. And this is what the classical price mechanism might be expected to bring about. A rise in rent and interest and a fall in wage-rates will induce producers to employ more labour with a given amount of land and capital if, but only if, a larger output can thereby be produced. No entrepreneur will take on more labour with a given amount of land and capital in order to produce a smaller or less-valuable total output. Indeed, it is one of the main merits of this use of the price mechanism that it will not choose inefficient techniques in order to make work for work's sake.

There can be little doubt that this principle is of the utmost relevance in an economy such as that of Mauritius. A few examples must suffice. In cane-fields weeding can be carried out either by hand or else in part at least, by the use of imported chemical herbicides. Which method it is profitable for the sugar estates to use depends essentially upon the wage and availability of labour. Another example is the handling of sugar when it has been produced. With the labour-intensive method, sugar is put into bags at the factory on the sugar estate, transported by rail or road to Port Louis, and carried by hand on to the ship, where the bag is opened and emptied into the ship's hold. The alternative capital-intensive method of bulk handling is to load the sugar automatically into special containers on road vehicles at the factory, to discharge the sugar from these vehicles automatically into silos at the quayside and to discharge the sugar automatically direct from the silos into the ship's hold at the quayside. This method economizes much labour in stevedoring at Port Louis, in handling the sugar in the factory and in the growing of the hemp and the manufacture of the hemp into bags, which is done at present at a government factory in Mauritius. On the other hand, it involves very heavy capital expenditure on the new road vehicles, on deepening the harbour to bring the ships to the quayside, on the new equipment at the port and so on. Whether or not it is the cheaper method depends essentially upon the wage-rate of labour compared with the cost of acquiring the necessary capital.

A further example is given by the problems involved in the establishment of a tea industry in Mauritius. Tea is a rather labour-intensive crop and needs a higher level of employment per acre than sugar. There are prospects that Mauritius might be able to produce good-quality tea. Just because tea is a rather labour-intensive crop it is very appropriate as a way of saving land and using labour. But just because it is a labour-intensive crop the wage element in its cost is of great importance. At present the wage-rate in Mauritius is significantly higher than in Ceylon and East Africa, with whose teas Mauritian tea would have to compete. The success of this new avenue for employment will be greatly affected by the cost of labour in Mauritius.

Mauritius will be able to find productive employment for a greatly increased working force only if she can establish and expand some manufacturing industries. She cannot rely on finding employment for a greatly increased population in her present staple industry, namely sugar. The sugar industry is a highly progressive one in which output per worker employed is constantly rising. The world market for sugar is at present strong; but even if the market for Mauritian sugar expands as rapidly as the output of Mauritian sugar, there is a strict limit to the amount of land on which sugar can be grown, and this must set a strict upper limit to employment in the sugar industry in Mauritius. Other lines of agricultural production are capable of some significant expansion; but in the end limitations of land will make it impossible to find sufficient employment in these lines of agricultural production.

Mauritius must develop some industries. But in manufacturing industry the island starts with many disadvantages. She has little technical knowhow in manufactures or experience, outside the sugar factories, in the conduct of industry; she has little technical training; she has few raw materials; she is not rich in capital; and her domestic market alone will not provide a sufficient market for large-scale production. She must emulate in a minor way economies such as Hong

Kong, Jamaica, Japan and the United Kingdom, where raw materials are imported to be made into manufactures for export. But can Mauritius establish such manufactures except on the basis of cheap labour? Initially, at least, plentiful labour will be her one comparative advantage.

While the simple classical answer would be to reduce the wage-rate in Mauritius, in fact in recent years exactly the opposite has happened. After a considerable period of stability, both of the cost of living and of the money wage-rate, between 1956 and 1959 the wage-rate in the sugar industry (which sets the pattern for the rest of the island) went up by some 45 per cent, while the cost of living remained constant. Here in a most marked form is the basic economic dilemma or paradox of such communities. The sugar industry was certainly very prosperous in the sense that the big sugar estates were making very good incomes from rents and profits, and the political awakening of the underdog in Mauritius has not unnaturally been associated with aggressive trade-union action, which has pushed up the wage-rate in the sugar industry as a method of redistributing part of the wealth of the island. But from the point of view of getting the best use of resources in Mauritius there is little doubt that the wage-rate ought to be very low.

Moreover, the effect of the wage-rate on the level of rents and profits in an economy like that of Mauritius will affect the rate of economic development in another way. In Mauritius the big sugar estates do in fact plough back a large part of their profits for the expansion of the sugar industry; the rate of profits tax is high, the rates of personal income tax on the higher incomes are high and progressive, and these direct taxes are collected by an efficient tax administration. The result is that a substantial part of the high gross profits and rents either goes direct into the capital development of the sugar industry or goes to swell the Government's budgetary revenue, from which capital development outside the sugar industry is largely financed by the State. A high wage-rate is also, therefore, liable to reduce the rate of economic development by reducing the sources of private and public capital accumulation.

This is perhaps the basic economic conundrum of such overpopulated underdeveloped countries. Let us take an extreme example and consider a country which is so overpopulated that if all available labour were employed the marginal product of labour would be zero. Then to get the most out of the country's resources and to maximize its national income labour should be free to all who want to use it. But, of course, if the wage-rate is set at zero, while the national income may be maximized it will all go in rents, interest, dividends and profits to the owners of property, and none of it will go to labour. If the wage-rate is set at a level which gives labour a reasonable share of the product, then there will be under-employment and unemployment; foreign capital will not be attracted as it might be by the high rate of profit which would result if the labour which it employed were freely available to it;[1] traditional labour-intensive processes and products will be discouraged; engineers and technicians, who in any case will normally have been trained in developed countries where the need is to save labour rather than capital, will not be encouraged to apply new scientific knowledge in devising new ways to enable much labour to work effectively with little capital equipment; the economy will not be able to compete as it should with foreign producers of labour-intensive products; and the sources of capital accumulation, and so of economic growth, may be dried up.

An underdeveloped economy like that of Mauritius with scarce resources of land and capital but threatened with intense overpopulation presents the conflict between efficiency and distribution in its most dramatic form—for economic

---

[1] The fact that in many underdeveloped countries the wage-rate is higher than it would be in full-employment competitive equilibrium may be one of the main reasons which explains the paradox that capital appears to be attracted for investment into developed countries such as the United States, the United Kingdom and Germany, where the ratio of capital to labour is already high, rather than into underdeveloped countries where the supply of capital is low relatively to that of labour. The return on capital in such underdeveloped countries would be much higher if the wage-rate were reduced to correspond to the marginal product of labour in conditions of full employment.

efficiency labour should be treated as if it cost nothing, but a zero wage rate would allot nearly all of the Mauritian national income to a few 'sugar barons'.

Up to this point I have spoken of the efficiency of an economic system in very static terms, that is to say, as if it were simply a question of using today's resources in such a way that it would be impossible to make anyone better off today without making someone else worse off today. But in fact, of course, much productive activity today will be making capital equipment which will be used to enhance someone's final consumption of goods and services tomorrow or the next day or the day after that. It would always be possible to make some citizens better off today without making any others worse off today by using more resources to produce for today's consumption and less resources to produce capital goods today which will be useful either to produce consumption goods tomorrow or to produce capital goods tomorrow which will be useful to produce consumption goods the day after tomorrow—and so on. If we consider an economy moving through time, we can say that it behaves in an efficient manner only if at each point of time it would be impossible to make some citizen better off at that point of time without making someone worse off at that same point of time or at some other point of time.

At any one point of time each individual producer in our economy will be faced with a set of prices at which he can sell any consumption goods (bread and shirts) which he chooses to make and a set of prices at which he can sell any capital goods (ploughs and looms) which he chooses to make. At the same time there will be a certain amount of resources (land, men, existing capital equipment) available to produce these various outputs—bread, shirts, ploughs, looms. Competition among the individual producers for the use of the available resources will bid up the price of each resource until it is profitable to use it only in the most efficient ways in the most productive uses. This will maximize the value of total output at the given selling prices of the various products. The competitive bidding up of the prices of the available productive resources will raise the cost of production of each product up to its selling price. It will be possible to produce £1-worth more bread only if £1-worth less shirts or ploughs or looms are produced.

The consequent use of resources will be a fully efficient one *provided that the future course of market prices and of technical production possibilities is correctly foreseen.* It is not possible to give on this occasion a precise proof of this formidable proposition; but it can be intuitively demonstrated in the following way.

As far as goods for immediate consumption are concerned (bread and shirts), the current market prices will measure their importance to consumers. It will not therefore be possible to make present consumers better off by producing £1-worth more shirts and £1-worth less bread or *vice versa*; they could only be made better off by producing less ploughs or less looms for future use, i.e. at the expense of citizens in the future.

It remains only to ask whether some future citizen might not be made better off without any other being made worse off by altering the composition of today's output of capital goods. Suppose, for example, that one plough costs the same to produce as one loom and that one more plough and one less loom were produced today for future use. This would alter the future flow of consumption goods onto the markets, more bread and less shirts being made available. Suppose that it were possible by such a change to keep all consumers at every point of time equally well off (the increased supply of bread having the same price at each future point of time as the decreased supply of shirts) except that at one point of time some one consumer could be made better off without any one else being made worse off (the increased supply of bread having at that point of time a higher price than the decreased supply of shirts). Suppose further that these market conditions and technical possibilities were correctly foreseen. Then an entrepreneur today would be prepared to offer a higher price for a plough than for a loom, because there would be a prospect of a higher return on the former than on the latter. More ploughs and less looms would be produced. The current use of resources would be drawn away from its inefficient pattern.

Thus in order to set today's prices in a pattern which will act as a guide to an efficient use of today's resources, one must know future technical production possibilities and the pattern of future prices. This requirement can, of course, never be perfectly fulfilled, though systematic co-operation (for example, in the National Economic Development Council) in comparing, co-ordinating, and assessing individual plans for future development may help to achieve more accurate expectations about future market conditions.

But in any case it remains true—and that is the essential point for our present purpose—that there may be most important divergences between the 'efficiency' and the 'distributional' aspects of pricing. The fact that an economy is developing through time complicates, in the way which we have just examined, the use of prices for efficiency purposes; but it in no way ensures that the prices which we reckon today to be the best guide to an efficient use of today's resources will result in a desirable distribution of today's income and wealth.

I have explained at some length what must be the characteristics of an economy which is moving efficiently through time. But such an efficient time path must be distinguished from what may be called the optimum time path. A time path is, as we have seen, efficient if as time passes it is always impossible to re-arrange today's use of resources so as to make some future consumers better off without making any other present or future consumers worse off. Suppose that the situation is continuously efficient in this sense. It still remains an open question whether it would not in fact be desirable to make future consumers better off even though this must be at the expense of present consumers. This could always be done by increasing today's savings so that less was spent by today's consumers on today's consumption goods and services and more was invested by today's citizens in new machines and other items of real capital equipment to be available to serve tomorrow's citizens. The optimum time path is that one among the infinite number of possible efficient time paths which

21

provides the most desirable distribution of real consumption between the consumers of different years.

In reality in the choice of economic policies there are four basic *desiderata* to be borne in mind:—

(1) First, it is desirable that resources should not be wasted in involuntary unemployment. Monetary policy (by making more difficult or more easy the terms on which money can be borrowed for the purchase of capital goods) and budgetary policy (by raising or lowering the amount of private spending power taken away in taxation or by lowering or raising the level of governmental expenditure on goods and services) can be used to reduce or to raise the level of total money expenditure on goods and services, so that the general level of demand for economic resources is kept in balance with the supply of such economic resources.

(2) Second, it is not only desirable that all scarce resources should be used to produce something that is wanted. It is also desirable that they should be used in a fully efficient manner in the sense already explained at length in this book.

(3) Third, it is desirable that there should be an equitable distribution of income and wealth between the citizens in the community at any one point of time.

(4) Fourth, it is desirable to achieve an optimum level of savings at each point of time, that is to say, as we have already explained, to achieve the most desirable distribution of real consumption as between the citizens of successive time periods in the economy's development.

This book is essentially concerned with possible clashes between *desiderata* (2) and (3) in the above list—between the use of the price mechanism to achieve economic efficiency and its use to achieve distributional justice. Throughout the rest of this book I shall simply assume that monetary and budgetary policies are in the aggregate so used that full employment is maintained. *Desideratum* (1) is simply assumed to be achieved.

Many of the measures which will subsequently be discussed in these pages will affect the level of savings. We cannot, therefore, simply neglect *desideratum* (4), even though there will be no systematic discussion of the optimum level of savings in this book. There is indeed some reason to suppose that individual citizens left to themselves will save less than is socially desirable, partly simply because they are short-sighted and partly because individuals, unlike the State, are mortal and do not give as much weight to the interests of future generations as they do to themselves. We shall, there-fore, in what follows occasionally make incidental references to the effects of various policies upon the level of savings, counting it as a loss if any policy tends to reduce the propor-tion of the national income which is saved and invested in capital equipment for the use of future generations.

We are now in a position to return to our main theme—the problem of the possible clashes between the 'efficiency' and the 'distributional' aspects of prices and, in particular, of the real wage rate. The possibility of such a clash in an economy which is developing through time can be clearly seen by considering a highly developed economy such as that of the United Kingdom. The clash may not be quite so stark as in an overpopulated underdeveloped economy such as that of Mauritius; but it exists none the less. In such an industrialized country at any one time there is an existing array of natural resources and fixed capital equipment—land of various qualities and situations, plant and machinery of various forms, some new, some old, some rigidly designed for one use in one industry, some flexible general purpose tools, and so on. At the same time there is an existing array of workers in the labour force some old, some young, some highly educated, others with little education, some rigidly trained for one purpose only, some with a general-purpose training, some unskilled, some clever, some stupid, some strong, some weak, some tied to one locality, some mobile, and so on. Given the relative demands for the products of the various activities (including as we have seen the present demands for capital goods as determined by what we hope are correct anticipations of future conditions) efficiency requires that the existing array of workers be spread over the existing array of land and capital equipment in such a way that the value of the additional product due to the use of a worker at one point is not less than the value of the additional product due to his employment at any other point in the system. Efficiency does not require that literally all existing acres and machines be necessarily used. If labour is scarce and land and machines plentiful, it may be desirable to use the limited labour only on the most efficient and productive acres and machines. A high wage rate which measures the shortage of labour will make it impossible to work the other acres and machines without making an out-of-pocket loss. The land is sub-marginal; the machines are obsolete. Perfection will, of course, never be reached. But a reasonable approach to this pattern of efficient use of men, machines, and natural resources requires the setting of today's prices or wage-rates for the various broad categories of labour at levels which will guide the various employers, public and private, to the most efficient use of the available labour.

As time passes some capital equipment will depreciate physically as a result of ageing and of wear and tear. Other and new equipment will have been built. Improved technical knowledge will have affected the capabilities of the new equipment and, to a lesser degree, of some of the old equipment as well. The size of the working population may have changed and the amount and quality of educational effort invested in the new members of the labour force may have increased. The efficient spreading of the new array of workers over the new array of equipment may well require some change in the level and pattern of real wage rates.

In a highly industrialised developed economy this process will generally entail a continuous rise in output per head. Net capital accumulation means that the machinery and plant which is newly installed will exceed the machinery and plant which is physically worn out; technical progress will raise output per worker employed; and increased investment in training and education will also raise the workers' productivity. Unless there is a very rapid rise in the size of the new working population to be spread over the new array of equipment, real output per head is likely to be higher. But as every professional economist knows output per head (the average product of labour) is not the same thing as the addition to output which is due to the employment of an additional amount of labour (the marginal product of labour). It is the latter and not the former which is relevant to the use of the real wage rate as a guide to the efficient use of resources. Indeed this is the very heart of our dilemma. It is the value of the additional product which could be produced by taking on a little more labour which should on efficiency grounds be related to the real wage rate; it is the value of total output per head which will determine the total real income available for distribution among all citizens. If the marginal product of labour is low but its average product is high, wages paid on our efficiency basis will represent only a small proportion of total real income, the remainder accruing to the owners of property in profits and rent.

In the highly developed industrialized countries a substantial proportion of the real product does accrue to the owners of property and property is very unequally owned. There is already, therefore, a problem. The pattern of real wage rates which is required on efficiency grounds may lead to a very high level of real income per head for the small concentrated number of rich property owners. And it is possible, though not certain, that this problem will become more acute as a result of automation.

To the engineer automation in industry means the incorporation into a productive process of a particular type of control mechanism. In the economists' jargon this implies, I suspect, a high rate of technical progress with a marked labour-saving bias in it. Automation will certainly increase the output per head which will be produced by the aid of the new automated machinery. But it could conceivably reduce so much the amount of labour needed with each new machine of a given cost that the total demand for labour was actually reduced. This could happen if, in spite of the net accumulation of capital equipment, the new labour required with the new automated machines was actually less than the growth of the labour force plus the labour made redundant by the scrapping

25

of physically worn-out old machinery. In such a case to absorb the new and the redundant workers in the next best uses (for example, on machinery previously considered obsolete or in uses which need no machinery such as domestic service) might require an absolute reduction in the real wage rate on efficiency grounds. Even if this extreme case were avoided, it is clear that automation might well cause output per head to rise relatively to the marginal product of labour. In this case efficiency pricing would require that an ever-increasing proportion of output accrued to property owners and the distributional dilemma would to this extent be intensified.

Most discussions about the social and economic problems which will arise in an automated world run in terms of the rise in real output and real income per head of the population. What, we ask, shall we all do with our leisure when we need to work only an hour or two a day to obtain the total output of real goods and services needed to satisfy our wants? But the problem is really much more difficult than that. The question which we should ask is: What shall we all do when output per man-hour of work is extremely high but practically the whole of the output goes to a few property owners, while the mass of the workers are relatively (or even absolutely) worse off than before?

II

The Present Position in the Developed Countries

The problem is already a very real one in the highly indus-trialized developed countries in many of which there is a really fantastic inequality in the ownership of property. As the figures in the following table[1] show, at the end of the 1950's in the United Kingdom, in spite of some marked equalization since pre-World War I, the ownership of private property

Table 1. *Distribution of Personal Wealth in the United Kingdom*

· Percentage of Population	Percentages of Total Personal Wealth			Percentages of Personal Income from Property (before Tax) 1959 ·
	1911–13	1936–38	1960	
1	69	56	42	60
5	87	79	75	92
10	92	88	83	99

was still extremely unequal. For example, no less than 75 per cent of personal property was owned by the wealthiest 5 per cent of the population. Moreover, the rich obtain a higher yield on their property than do the poor, presumably partly because they are better informed through financial advisers but partly because with larger properties risks can be taken and spread more easily so that the average yield is higher. The result is that the concentration of income from property is even more marked than the concentration of property

[1] I am indebted to Mr. J. R. S. Revell of the Department of Applied Economics of the University of Cambridge for these figures.

ownership itself, and in 1959 no less than 92 per cent of income from property went to 5 per cent of the population.[1]

What effect this concentration will have upon the distribution of total incomes between persons will depend upon two other proportions. (i) The first of these is the proportion of total personal incomes which is made up of income from property; if this proportion is small, then a very unequal distribution of property will not in itself lead to any great inequality in the distribution of total income; it is when 'efficiency' demands that only a small proportion of income should be paid in wages, leaving much to accrue in profits, interest, and rents that the inequality in the ownership of property causes great inequalities in the distribution of income. (ii) The other factor is the distribution of earned incomes; if the rich owners of property cannot earn more than the average wage per head, earned incomes will reduce the inequalities due to property incomes; but if the earnings of the rich are also as concentrated as their unearned incomes, there will be no diminution of inequalities of income from this source.

The interaction between these various factors can be shown by a set of formulae of the following kind:—

$$i_1 = p_1 (1 - q) + l_1 q$$
$$i_5 = p_5 (1 - q) + l_5 q$$
$$i_{10} = p_{10} (1 - q) + l_{10} q$$

Let q represent the proportion of total personal income which is paid in earnings so that $1 - q$ represents the proportion going in income on property. If p_1 represents the proportion of total income from property going to the 1 per cent of the population who receive the largest total incomes and l_1 represents the proportion of earned incomes which are received by the same 1 per cent of the population with the highest total

---

[1] The figures for the concentration of property ownership and those for the concentration of income from property are not strictly comparable, since in the former the population relates to all individuals over 25 in England and Wales while in the latter it refers to the total number of income-tax units in the United Kingdom.

incomes, then $p_1 (1 - q)$ will represent the proportion of total personal incomes which accrues to this group in the form of unearned incomes and $l_1 q$ will represent the proportion of the total of personal incomes which accrues to this group in the form of earnings. Thus $p_1 (1 - q) + l_1 q$ or i_1 will equal the proportion of total personal incomes accruing to the 1 per cent of the population with the highest total incomes. Similarly i_5 and i_{10}, p_5 and p_{10}, and l_5 and l_{10} represent these proportions for the richest 5 per cent and the richest 10 per cent of the population.

Table 2. Distribution of Personal Incomes from Property and Earnings, United Kingdom, 1959

Percentage of Population	Percentage of Personal Incomes from Property (p)	Percentage of Personal Incomes from Earnings (l)	Percentage of Total Personal Incomes (i)		
			$q = 95\%$	$q = 85\%$	$q = 75\%$
1	47	6	8	12	16
5	66	17	19	24	29
10	73	27	29	34	38

For the United Kingdom in 1959 we can very roughly estimate the p's and l's as is done in Table 2.[1] For the reasons given in Appendix I it is more difficult to estimate the relevant value for q, but the last three columns of Table 2 give the values of i which would result if q were 95, 85, or 75 per cent respectively. These figures give some indication of the importance of q in determining the distribution of total personal

[1] For the source of these figures see Appendix I (pp. 78–81 below). It is to be noted that the figures in the last column of Table 1 (p. 27) differ from those for (p) in Table 2 because the former show the percentages of income from property accruing to the persons who have the largest incomes *from property* whereas the latter show the percentages of income from property accruing to persons who have the largest incomes *from all sources*. Thus in Table 2 the richest citizens include some who have very high earnings but not such high incomes from property. Income from property is necessarily more concentrated in Table 1 than in Table 2. The figures in Table 2 show the distribution of incomes before equalization through taxation.

29

incomes. Thus with q equal to 85 per cent the richest 5 per cent of the population would receive 24 per cent of total personal incomes, made up of 66 per cent of total personal incomes from property and 17 per cent of total incomes from earnings. The distribution of earned income is much more equal than that of income from property. If q were lowered by automation from 85 to 75 per cent, then the richest 5 per cent of the population (with the same distribution of income from property and the same distribution of income from earnings, i.e. with the p's and l's unchanged) would receive 29 per cent instead of 24 per cent of total personal incomes. The unequally distributed incomes from property would have become more important relatively to the less unequally distributed incomes from work.

The above account is in one way very incomplete, if not positively misleading. Earning power depends upon education and training, and education and training involve the investment of scarce resources in those who are educated and trained. This represents an important form of capital and of property; and a considerable part of the earnings of the educated and trained is in fact a return on the capital invested in their education. This form of capital is not recognised in Tables 1 and 2 above, where personal property includes only the tangible marketable assets of a person and excludes the intangible unmarketable value of his education and where earned income includes all the increase in earnings which are due to the capital invested in education and training. In a highly developed industrialized country the total value of the capital sunk in the education of the population can be very great as is illustrated by the figures in Table 3[1] for the United States of America.

The figures in lines 2 and 3 of this table measure the value of the resources (teachers' salaries, costs of running the schools, etc.) directly used up in the past education of the existing citizens of the country. They also include, as they should, in the case of the later stages of education, the wage

[1] These figures are taken from Theodore W. Schultz *The Economic Value of Education*, p. 51.

earnings foregone by the students as a result of staying on at School or University instead of earning their living more promptly. Such is a true capital investment; immediate income is sacrificed for future benefit. When earnings foregone are thus included in the capital cost of an education, the total cost of the later stages of education is greatly increased. From Table 3 it can be seen that in 1957 the capital sunk in the

Table 3. *The Stock of Tangible and Intangible Capital in the United States, 1929 and 1957*

	1929	1957
	($000,000,000 of 1956 value)	
1. Reproducible tangible wealth	727	1270
2. Educational capital in population as a whole, of which	317	848
3. Educational capital in labour force ..	173	535

education of the total population represented 40 per cent of the total of physical tangible capital plus intangible educational capital.[1]

Of course expenditure on education cannot be treated simply as any other form of productive capital investment. It confers benefits quite apart from the fact that it increases the future commercial earning power of the educated. It enables the educated person to enjoy a fuller life quite apart from any increase in his money income which it may bring; and it has further social advantages in that in many ways it is better for his neighbours to live with him as an educated rather than as an uneducated fellow citizen. But education does undoubtedly have value to the educated person as a straightforward commercial investment. It increases the productivity and economic value of the person educated. There is considerable evidence that, even if we make no allowance for the general cultural and social advantages of education, the return

_____

[1] Even if one confined one's attention to the capital sunk in the education of the labour force, this percentage would still be 30 per cent.

on it as a purely commercial proposition is very high, particularly in the case of the spread of elementary education among a previously largely uneducated community.[1]

There has in the last half century been an enormous increase in the amount of education per citizen in the developed countries of the world.[2] To what extent this is a force equalizing the ownership of property and earnings depends upon two factors: (1) Has the additional educational investment been received by those who are already wealthy or by those who are poor? (2) Who has provided the cost of the education invested in these persons?

There can be no doubt that the great expansion of the first stages of education in the last half century has been an equalizing factor of the greatest importance. It has been financed by taxation which has fallen presumably at least somewhat more heavily on the rich than on the poor and it has been open without direct charge to the poor. If the figures of personal property and of income from personal property in Tables 1 and 2 could be recast to include the intangible stock of educational capital invested in each person and that part of his earnings which was a return on this investment, there would have been revealed undoubtedly a greater movement away from extreme inequalities in property ownership and in incomes from property.

But we cannot in fact arrange our figures in such a way as to include educational capital in personal property; and educational capital has so many peculiar features that we should perhaps in any case not wish to do so. In what follows we

---

[1] Theodore W. Schultz *op. cit.* p. 62 mentions rates of return of 35 per cent per annum on elementary education, 10 per cent per annum on high school education, and 11 per cent per annum on college education for the United States of America in 1959.

[2] Theodore W. Schultz *op. cit.* p. 50 gives an estimate of a rise in the number of years of schooling completed per person from 4·14 in 1900 to 10·45 in 1957 in the United States of America. Since the later years of schooling are so much more expensive than the early years of elementary school, the cost of capital sunk in education per person has gone up even more markedly between 1900 and 1957 from $2,236 to $7,555 (dollars of constant 1956 purchasing power).

shall consider personal property as referring only to tangible assets and we shall treat educational investment in a special category as something which has a special effect upon the capacity to earn income.

We have already noted that the ratio q, namely the proportion of the national income that accrues to wages is an essential factor which decides the importance of the distribution of property ownership in determing the distribution of income. The really overpopulated underdeveloped economy is one in which on efficiency grounds q should be practically zero, in which case income distribution would be wholly determined by the distribution of income from property. In the United Kingdom at the present q is perhaps about 85 per cent and the distribution of income thus depends much less on the distribution of property and much more on the distribution of earning power.

But what of the future? Suppose that automation should drastically reduce q. The country would tend to become a wealthy edition of Mauritius. There would be a limited number of exceedingly wealthy property owners; the proportion of the working population required to man the extremely profitable automated industries would be small; wage rates would thus be depressed; there would have to be a large expansion of the production of the labour-intensive goods and services which were in high demand by the few multi-multi-multi-millionaires; we would be back in a super-world of an immiserized proletariat and of butlers, footmen, kitchen maids, and other hangers-on. Let us call this the Brave New Capitalists' Paradise.

It is to me a hideous outlook. What could we do about it? The rest of these pages will be devoted to a discussion of four possible lines of attack which we may summarize as the replacement of the Brave New Capitalists' Paradise by

(1) A Trade Union State.
(2) A Welfare State.
(3) A Property-Owning Democracy.
(4) A Socialist State.

c

I shall deal with the first two of these very briefly and cursorily because the problems connected with them are familiar to most economists. My present purpose is to recommend for much closer attention and study the last two modes of a Property-Owning Democracy and of a Socialist State.

III

The Trade Union State

By trade union action or by legislation a minimum real wage might be set for all work done. The outstanding disadvantage of this form of action is that it would reduce the volume of employment that it was profitable to provide with a given amount of real capital equipment. It is possible, but not certain, that automation involves not only (i) a rise in output per man and (ii) a reduction in the relative importance of men to machines but also (iii) a reduction in the elasticity of substitution between men and machines. If this is so, the direct damage done by the pushing up of the wage rate in any one automated industry would be limited; if a fixed number of men is required to look after each automated machine, a rise in the real wage will cause a fall in profits without much affect on employment per machine.

But this does not mean to say that the damage done to the economy as a whole would be slight. Automation is a matter of degree. There would be many industries where the ratio of men to machines was neither rigid nor low. In industries in which the ratio of men to machines was not rigid the 'inefficiently' high real wage would restrict the demand for men per machine, and in industries in which the ratio of men to machines was not low the cost of the product would rise relatively to the cost of the fully-automated machine-intensive products. The labour-intensive industries (including of course above all the occupations for personal service) would be contracted relatively to other industries. The total demand for labour would be reduced.

There would then be three possibilities.

(i) The first possibility is that the minimum wage arrangements are in fact operative only in a limited number of fully automated industries and occupations. Society would then be divided into three economic classes: the very wealthy property owners, the privileged workers who were lucky enough to get the limited number of available posts in the protected occupations, and the underprivileged workers whose wage would be extremely low as they competed for the remaining jobs. The minimum wage protection in the privileged jobs would reduce not only the profits of the capitalists but also the real wages of the unprivileged workers in so far as it led to any restriction of the number of jobs in the protected occupations; for this would increase the competition for jobs in the unprotected occupations.

(ii) The second possibility is that the minimum wage arrangements would be effectively extended to cover all occupations. By this I mean not merely that a given minimum *money* wage rate is extended throughout the economy, but that this minimum money wage rate effectively represents a minimum real wage rate. This means, of course, that we must abandon our present monetary and budgetary policies for full employment. The Trade Unions push up money wage rates on equity-distributional grounds. That is their basic *raison d'etre*. They succeed in pushing wage rates up more quickly than the rise in labour's marginal productivity. At present our financial authorities, in the interests of full employment, allow an expansion of total demand so that selling prices chase costs up in a vicious spiral of inflation. Real wage rates are not in fact raised more quickly than marginal productivity; but employment is maintained. This combination of policies would have to be abandoned. When money wage rates are pushed up, monetary demand must not be expanded by monetary and budgetary policy so as to maintain full employment; for we must avoid the raising of money selling prices of goods and services which would merely reduce the real wage rate again to the extent necessary to provide full employment. In other words the possibility which we are now examining involves the employment of a limited number of the working population at what is regarded as a fair real wage rate and the acceptance of unemployment for the remainder. This unemployment might be designated as the technological unemployment due to automation and labour-saving inventions.

(iii) The third possibility is that an effective arrangement for the universal application of a minimum real wage should be combined with an effective limitation of the amount of work which any one individual citizen might do. Such work sharing—or might one not more appropriately call it such unemployment-sharing?—might be effected partly by preventing some potential workers (e.g. the young, the old, and the married women) from working at all, partly by limiting the number of hours which any worker might work, and partly by a network of trade union restrictive practices which spread each job over an unnecessarily large number of workers—the modern form of Luddite activity. This possibility would certainly be better than those previously described: it could in the conditions envisaged effectively raise the incomes of workers relatively to those of property earners without creating an underprivileged class of deprived workers or a solid mass of unemployed workers. But it is nevertheless an inefficient system and might turn out to be a very inefficient system. For it means partly that an artificial technical inefficiency is created by various restrictive practices and partly that there is an artificial edict against the provision of those labour-intensive products and services which workers (who are by hypothesis being forced to work less than they would like to do at the current wage rate) would like to produce for other workers (who would buy these services if only they were cheaper).

IV

The Welfare State

By this I mean the taxation of the incomes of the rich to subsidize directly or indirectly the incomes of the poor. I shall not describe the many possible variants of this principle. The whole system is one which is much discussed these days and with which we are all fairly familiar. In my view it could have one great and decisive advantage over the Trade Union—Minimum-Wage method. It could be combined with a real wage rate which was as low as considerations of efficiency demanded, so that labour-intensive activities were in no way inhibited; but at the same time the gross inequalities of income that would otherwise result would be avoided. There would remain, however, two defects in the system, (i) one from the point of view of efficiency and (ii) the other from the point of view of distribution.

(i) If, in the automated world we are envisaging, a really substantial equalization of individual incomes is to be achieved solely by redistributive income taxes and subsidies, the rates of income tax would have to be quite exceptionally progressive; and such highly progressive income taxation is bound to affect adversely incentives to work, save, innovate, and take risks. This subject is a controversial but nevertheless familiar one. I do not wish to develop it in these pages. The system unquestionably involves inefficiencies, though it may be debatable how great those inefficiencies would be.

(ii) The system could be used to equalize incomes; but it would not directly equalize property ownership. Extreme inequalities in the ownership of property are in my view undesirable quite apart from any inequalities of income which they may imply. A man with much property has great bargaining strength and a great sense of security, independence, and freedom; and he enjoys these things not only *vis-à-vis* his propertyless fellow citizens but also *vis-à-vis* the public authorities. He can snap his fingers at those on whom he must rely for an income; for he can always live for a time on his capital. The propertyless man must continuously and without interruption acquire his income by working for an employer or by qualifying to receive it from a public authority. An unequal distribution of property means an unequal distribution of power and status even if it is prevent from causing too unequal a distribution of income.

V

<hr />

A Property-Owning Democracy

Let us suppose that by the wave of some magic wand—the nature of which we will examine later—the ownership of property could be equally distributed over all the citizens in the community. What a wonderful culture could now result from our future automated economy! Imagine a world in which no citizen owns an excessively large or an unduly small proportion of the total of private property. Each citizen will now be receiving a large part of his income from property. For we are assuming that for society as a whole the proportion of income which accrues from earnings has been greatly reduced by automation. Institutions in the capital market would no doubt need to be appropriately developed so that a very large number of moderate private properties could be pooled through insurance companies, investment trusts, and similar intermediaries so that risks were spread and the ultimate investments chosen by specialists on behalf of the man in the street.

The essential feature of this society would be that work had become rather more a matter of personal choice. The unpleasant work that had to be done would have to be very highly paid to attract to it those whose tastes led them to wish to supplement considerably their incomes from property. At the other extreme those who wished to devote themselves to quite uncommercial activities would be able to do so with a reduced standard of living, but without starving in a garret. Above all labour-intensive services would flourish of a kind which (unlike old-fashioned domestic service) might be produced by one man for another man of equal income and status. Play-acting, ballet-dancing, painting, writing, sporting activities and all such 'unproductive' work as Adam Smith would have called it would flourish on a semi-professional semi-amateur basis; and those who produced such services would no longer be degraded as the poor sycophants of immoderately rich patrons.

Let us turn our attention therefore to the questions why in the sort of free-enterprise or mixed economy with which we are familiar we end up with such startling inequalities in the ownership of property, what changes in our institutional or tax arrangements would be necessary substantially to equalize ownership, and what disadvantages from the point of view of efficiency these reforms could themselves have.

I shall consider these matters in three stages. First, I shall assume that we are dealing simply with a number of adult citizens who have presumably been born in the past but who do not marry or have children or die or even grow old in the sense of experiencing diminished ability or vigour as time passes. I shall at this first stage examine the effects upon property distribution as these citizens work, save, and accumulate property. I shall assume that the State taxes neither income nor property and does not interfere in any way with this process of private capital accumulation.

At a second stage I shall introduce the demographic factors—births, marriages, deaths—and will examine the way in which they are likely to modify the pattern of ownership that would otherwise be developing.

At the third stage I will introduce the State. At this stage we shall be concerned with the ways in which economic and financial policies might be devised to modify the economic and demographic factors in such a way as to lead to a more equal distribution of property.

For the first stage I will employ a method which has been pioneered for another purpose by my colleague Dr. L. Pasinetti.[1] Consider two personal properties a small one (K_1) and

[1] In the 'Rate of Profit and Income Distribution in relation to the Rate of Economic Growth' (*Review of Economic Studies* Volume XXIX No. 4) Dr. Pasinetti assumes two classes of persons: workers who save a low

a large one (K_2). Will the small property be growing at a smaller or a larger proportional rate of growth than the large property? If the small property is growing at a greater proportional rate (say, 5 per cent per annum) than the large property (say, 2 per cent per annum), then the ratio of $\dfrac{K_1}{K_2}$ will be becoming more nearly equal to unity. In this case *relative* inequality will be diminishing.[1] We are concerned then at this first stage of our enquiry with the factors which will determine the proportional rate of growth of different properties.

These proportional growth rates (which we will call k_1 and k_2) for our two properties may be expressed as

$$k_1 = \frac{S_1(E_1 + V_1 K_1)}{K_1} \quad \text{and} \quad k_2 = \frac{S_2(E_2 + V_2 K_2)}{K_2}$$

respectively, where E_1 and E_2 represent the earned incomes or wages of the two property owners and V_1 and V_2 represent the two rates of profit earned by the two owners on their properties K_1 and K_2. Thus $V_1 K_1$ and $V_2 K_2$ represent the unearned incomes of the two property owners and $E_1 + V_1 K_1$ and $E_2 + V_2 K_2$ their earned and unearned incomes. If S_1 and S_2

proportion of their income and capitalists who do no work but save a high proportion of their income. Since workers save, they also accumulate property; and Dr. Pasinetti is concerned with the distribution of property between workers and capitalists which will result from this dual process of capital accumulation as time passes. His object is to consider the ultimate steady-state ratio between savings and profits in order to use this relationship for the theory of economic growth. In an article by myself on 'The Rate of Profit in a Growing Economy' (*Economic Journal*, December 1963) I criticized some of Dr. Pasinetti's assumptions but suggested that the Pasinetti process, with certain modifications of assumptions about the distribution of earning power and about propensities to save, might serve as a powerful instrument in analysing the forces affecting the distribution of the ownership of property. It is this application of the Pasinetti process which is the subject of the present section of this book.

[1] *Absolute* inequality (i.e. K_2-K_1) might, of course, be increasing; but t is, I think *relative* inequality which should concern us most. That one property should be £10,000 greater than another may be of great importance when K_1 is £1,000 and K_2 is £11,000 and of very little importance if K_1 is £100,000 and K_2 £110,000.

represent the proportions of these incomes which are saved and added to accumulated property, then $S_1(E_1 + V_1 K_1)$ and $S_2 (E_2 + V_2 K_2)$ are the absolute annual increases in the two properties and these, expressed as a ratio of the two properties measure their proportionate rates of growth.

In these pages I can do little more than enumerate the various influences at work. Some of them, it will be seen, tend to make $k_1 > k_2$ (these are the equalizing tendencies), and some tend to make $k_2 > k_1$ (these are the disequalizing tendencies). There is undoubtedly at work a large element of these latter disequalizing tendencies—what Professor Myrdal has called the principle of Circular and Cumulative Causation —the 'to-him-that-hath-shall-be-given' principle. On the other hand, trees do not grow up to the skies, and there are some systematic equalizing tendencies. It is the balance between these equalizing and disequalizing factors which results in the end in a given unequal, but not indefinitely unequal, distribution of properties. Let us consider in turn the influences of E, V, and S upon the rate of growth of property k.

(1) The influence of earned incomes, E, must be an equalizing factor so far as two properties at the extreme ranges of the scale of properties are concerned. We can see the point this way. If K_1 were zero, citizen 1 would have only an earned income E_1. If he saved any part of this, his savings would be $S_1 E_1$ and his proportionate rate of accumulation of property would be $\dfrac{S_1 E_1}{0} = \infty$. Consider at the other extreme a multi-multi-multi-millionaire. Now earning power, E_1 may well be enhanced by the ownership of property, but not without limit. In the case of our multi-multi-multi-millionaire, E_2 will be negligible relatively to K_2. If $\dfrac{E_2}{K_2}$ were for practical purposes zero, k_2 would equal $\dfrac{S_2 V_2 K_2}{K_2} = S_2 V_2$. As between the extreme ranges then, we have $k_1 > k_2$ and there is bound to be equalization. This is perhaps the basic reason why our measure

43

of relative inequality $\dfrac{K_1}{K_2}$ can never reach zero or infinity. In the intermediate ranges all we can say is that the higher is $\dfrac{E}{K}$, the more rapid the rate of growth of property k, other things being equal. If earning power were equally distributed among our citizens (with $E_1 = E_2$), then this factor would be an equalizing one as between any two properties K_1 and K_2.

$$k_1 = S_1 \frac{E_1}{K_1} + S_1 V_1 \quad \text{and} \quad k_2 = S_2 \frac{E_2}{K_2} + S_2 V_2$$

If $S_1 = S_2$, $E_1 = E_2$, and $V_1 = V_2$, then $k_1 > k_2$ if $K_1 < K_2$.

(2) The factor V, on the other hand, is unquestionably disequalizing—at least in the United Kingdom where there is strong evidence that the rate of return on property is much lower for small properties than for large properties.[1] This is so even if one does not take into account capital gains; but, of course, capital gains should be included in the return on capital. Since the wealthy in the United Kingdom at least invest on tax grounds for capital gains rather than for income, the inclusion of capital gains in V_2 and V_1 would make the excess of V_2 over V_1 even more marked; and this is clearly an influence which will raise k_2 above k_1.[2] It is probable that there will be little difference in the V which is relevant for all properties above a certain range. It is doubtful whether the multi-millionaire can get any higher yield than the millionaire on his property. But as between the really small properties and the large range of big properties, this influence is likely to be

[1] See Table 1 (p. 27 above). It will be remembered that at this stage we are dealing with incomes before tax is deducted.

[2] The influence of capital gains could be even more marked than is implied in the text. Suppose that property owners regard as their income only the income paid out on their property and save a fraction of this, but in addition automatically accumulate 100 per cent of any capital gain not paid out in dividend or rent or interest. Then the formula for k becomes

$$k = S\frac{E}{K} + SV + V'$$ where V is the paid-out rate of return on capital and V' is the rate of return from capital gains. An excess of V'_2 over V'_1 will have an even more marked effect than an equal excess of V_2 over V_1 in raising k_2 above k_1.

disequalizing and to be a factor enabling the whole range of large properties to grow more rapidly than the small.

(3) Finally, what is the influence of S, the proportion of income saved, on k for different sizes of K? Economists have done a great deal of theoretical and statistical work on the factors determining the proportions of income saved and spent. These investigations are of basic importance not only for theories of employment and of growth (i.e. for the determination of the 'multiplier' and of the relationships between the rate of profit, the rate of growth, and the capital-output ratio) but also for the determination of the distribution among individuals of the ownership of property.

Let us consider only the implications of two possible features of a probable type of savings function.[1] Let us assume (i) that the proportion of income saved rises with a rise in real income, though not, of course, without limit, since less than 100 per cent of income will be saved however great is income, and (ii) that the proportion of income saved out of any given income falls the larger is the property owned. This second assumption means that a man with £1,000 a year all earned will save more than a man with £1,000 a year which represents the interest on a property of £10,000. For the ability to save will be the same, but the need to accumulate some property will be higher in the first than in the second case.

If the savings function is of this general form, then as between two unequal properties $(K_2 > K_1)$ owned by two persons with the same earning power $(E_1 = E_2)$, we cannot, without more precise information, say which will be growing the more rapidly. The fact that a larger total income will be enjoyed by the man with the larger property will tend to raise the proportion of income which he can save; but, on the other hand, the fact that he already has a larger property will tend to reduce the proportion of income which he will save, and, in addition, the fact that $\dfrac{E}{K}$ is low in his case will

[1] Strong evidence for the importance of these factors in the savings function is given in Richard Stone 'Private Saving in Britain: Past, Present and Future'. The Manchester School, May, 1964.

keep down the rate of growth of his property. (See pp. 43–44 above).

But with the sort of savings function which we are assuming there are two other kinds of comparison which one can make with more definite results. If one compares two citizens with equal incomes but unequal properties, the small property of the man with the high earning power will be growing the more rapidly; he has the same ability to save but a greater need to accumulate; his savings will be greater and his existing property smaller. If one compares two citizens with the same property, but different incomes, the property of the man with the high income (i.e. the high earning power) will be growing the more rapidly; he has a higher ability to save and the same need to accumulate; his savings will be greater and his existing property the same. The result is, of course, that with our assumed savings function there will be exceptionally strong forces at work associating high properties with high earning power. This combination of forces will exaggerate the inequality in the distribution of total personal incomes.[1]

Let us pass to the second stage of our examination of the factors determining the distribution of property, namely the demographic factors. Consider two citizens, man and wife, each with a property. The rate of growth of their properties is determined by the economic factors we have just considered—S, E, V, and K. They have children. These children grow up and start to earn and to save—they acquire E's and S's of their own. They start to accumulate properties of their own, at first at indefinitely high proportional rates of growth, since they start with no property. At some time both parents die and leave their properties to their children. The children at some time—it may be before or after their parents' deaths—choose spouses. And so two citizens and two properties join together in holy matrimony and restart the same process of marriage, birth, and death.

[1] These processes of accumulation and their effects upon the distribution of property are examined more technically in Appendix II below (pp. 82-87).

What we want to consider is whether the factors of marriage, birth, and death will lead to a greater or a lesser degree of concentration of property ownership than would have occurred through the processes of capital accumulation which we examined at stage one in the absence of marriage, births, and deaths. The answer depends upon two things: the degree of assortative mating and the degree of differential fertility.

Suppose that any man was equally likely to be married to any woman in our society. Suppose, that is to say, that there were no assortative mating. Then the cycle of birth, marriage, and death would introduce an important equalizing factor into the system. Let us isolate for examination this basic demographic factor by assuming for the moment that every married couple reproduces itself by producing one son and one daughter and then leaves half the joint property of the parents to each child. Consider in this context the wealthiest family in the community, i.e. the family which has the highest joint property of husband and wife; they have a son and a daughter who, if they married each other, would perpetuate the same extreme concentration of wealth which they inherited from their parents; but brother and sister do not marry each other; the rich son must marry a wife with less inherited property than himself and the rich daughter a husband with less inherited property than herself; they in turn have children who are not so much enriched by inheritance as they themselves were. The general reshuffle generation by generation through marriage tends to equalize inherited fortunes. If there were no assortative mating, there would be a strong probability that a citizen whose inheritance was exceptionally high would marry someone with a smaller inheritance and that a citizen whose inheritance was exceptionally low would marry someone with a larger inheritance. But of course in fact marriage is strongly assortative. The rich are brought up in the same social milieu as the rich, and the poor in the same social milieu as the poor. The reshufflement of property ownership is very much less marked.

Differential fertility could clearly have an important influence on the distribution of property. If rich parents had fewer children than did poor parents, the large fortunes would become more and more concentrated in fewer and fewer hands. If the rich had more children than the poor, the large properties would fall in relative size as they become more and more widely dispersed and the smaller would grow in relative size as they become more and more concentrated on a smaller number of children. At first sight it might, therefore, appear as if differential fertility might work in either direction— equalizing property ownership if the rich were exceptionally fertile and disequalizing it if the rich were exceptionally infertile. And this would, of course, be so in the short run; and it would be so in the long run as well, if there were some forces at work which caused riches itself to lead to exceptionally high or exceptionally low fertility.

But consider another possible type of cause of differential fertility. Suppose (i) that every couple has at least one child, but (ii) that there is some genetic factor at work which makes some couples more fertile than others and (iii) that this genetic factor is in no way correlated positively or negatively with any other relevant genetic characteristic. We may happen to start with the infertile at the bottom end of the property scale; if so, the immediate effect will be to tend to equalize property ownership. But gradually as time passes the infertile will be found, through the process of concentrated inheritance, further and further up the property scale. In the end it will be the rich who are the infertile and the poor who are the fertile. The permanent influence of such a form of differential fertility will thus ultimately be disequalizing in its effect upon property ownership.

But sons and daughters are endowed not only with inherited property but also with earning power. Here we are confronted with the great problem of nature *versus* nurture. Earning power undoubtedly depends largely upon environmental factors. We have already observed (pp. 30-32) the great importance of investment in education in raising earning power. In a society which (as we are assuming in this second stage of our enquiry) left everything including education to private market forces rich fathers could educate their sons much more readily than could poor fathers. The inheritance of a good education would be just like the inheritance of tangible wealth from rich parents.

But high earning power is not wholly due to education and other environmental factors; there can be no doubt that there are also some genetic factors at work in determining a person's ability to earn. In so far as this is the case, there may be a social mechanism at work analogous to, although not identical with, the mechanism which some scholars have suspected to be at work in the case of social class and intelligence.[1] Let us very briefly outline this mechanism in the case of social class and intelligence and then point the possible analogy with property and earning power.

Suppose that whatever quality it may be which is measured by an intelligence test is a quality which enables one to succeed in modern life, so that there is some tendency for the intelligent to move up, and the unintelligent to move down, the social scale. Then at any one time one would expect to find a positive correlation between intelligence and social class; the more intelligent citizens will tend to be found with greater frequency at the top of the social ladder. Suppose further that whatever is measured by an intelligence test is a quality which has at least *some* genetic element in its causation. One would in that case expect to find some positive correlation, but a less than perfect correlation, between the intelligence of parents and the intelligence of their children. The children of intelligent parents would tend to be intelligent but not as intelligent as their parents; the children of unintelligent parents would tend to be unintelligent but not as unintelligent as their parents. This 'regression towards the mean' is to be explained by the fact that an intelligent father, transmitting only one of each of his chromosome pairs to his son, will on the average transmit only one half of the genes which made him exceptionally intelligent. The son of such a father has a higher chance than the average of being exceptionally intelligent, but on the

[1] See Michael Young and John Gibson. 'In Search of an Explanation of Social Mobility', *British Journal of Statistical Psychology*, XVI, 27-36.

average is not likely to be as exceptionally intelligent as his father.[1]

As the following figures show, this is the pattern which in fact one finds.[2]

Table 4. Mean I.Q.s of Parent and Child According to Class of Parents

				Parent	Child
Higher Professional	..	..	..	139.7	120.8
Lower Professional	..	..	..	130.6	114.7
Clerical	..	..	..	115.9	107.8
Skilled	..	..	..	108.2	104.6
Semi-skilled	..	..	..	97.8	98.9
Unskilled	..	..	..	84.9	92.6
Average	..	..	..	100.0	100.0

Column 1 shows how intelligence is higher, the higher the citizen concerned stands on the social scale. Column 2 shows the 'regression towards the mean'. The most (least) intelligent parents have children with above-average (below-average) intelligence, but not so much above-average (below-average) as the parents. The genetic 'regression towards the mean' tends to equalize the distribution of intelligence between social classes; but social mobility upwards of those children whose intelligence happens by the luck of the genetic draw to be high relatively to the social class of their parents, and mobility downwards for those children whose intelligence happens to be low relatively to the social class of their parents, restores the original association between class and intelligence displayed in the parents' generation.

Such is the hypothesis. If we had the figures and could draw up a similar table for property ownership and earning ability, would we find the same kind of relationship? It is possible that by the mechanism of accumulation already described (that is to say, because high earning power makes it easier to accumulate property) there is some positive corre-

[1] See C. O. Carter, *Human Heredity* pp. 103-4.
[2] These figures are quoted from Sir Cyril Burt 'Intelligence and Social Mobility' (*British Journal of Statistical Psychology*, XIV, 3-25) by Michael Young and John Gibson *op. cit.* p. 29.

lation between large properties and high earning power. But if earning power is to some extent genetically determined, one would expect to find rich parents with high earning power having children with above-average earning power, but not so much above-average as themselves; and one would expect to find the poorest parents with the lowest earning power having children with below-average earning power but not so much below average as themselves. But the association between property ownership and earning power may nevertheless be restored in the next generation by the exceptionally rapid

	Earning power of	
	Owners	Children of Owners
Very large properties	?	?
Large properties	?	?
Medium properties..	?	?
Small properties	?	?
Very small properties	?	?

accumulation of property by those children who happen to be born with exceptionally high earning power relatively to their inherited property and by the exceptionally slow rate of accumulation by those children to happen to be born with exceptionally low earning power relatively to their inherited property.

All that one can say in the present unhappy state of almost complete ignorance about this important aspect of society is that in so far as earning power is a factor which leads to the accumulation of property, then any 'regression towards the mean' in the inheritance of earning power would in itself tend to equalize the distribution of the ownership of property.[1]

[1] The preceding paragraphs suggest that (i) low fertility and (ii) high ability to earn may both be factors which tend to raise people upon the social scale and the property ladder. These factors probably both have some genetic elements in their determination. Moreover, it is a well-known fact that men and women are likely to marry within their own class. Thus there may be a continuous process tending to mate the genes for ability with those for infertility and the genes for inability with those for fertility. The dysgenic aspect of such a social arrangement is obvious. (cf. Professor R. A. Fisher. *The Social Selection of Human Fertility*, pp. 22-32).

We have so far considered some of the economic and biological factors which may systematically work towards the equalization or the disequalization of the ownership of property. But there are, of course, for any individual enormously important elements of pure environmental luck. Was a man lucky or unlucky in the actual school to which he went as a child and in the actual teachers which he there encountered? Was he lucky or unlucky in the actual locality in which he sought work or took his business initiatives? Was he lucky or unlucky in the choice of the subject matter of his education and training? In the choice of industries in which he invested his first savings or initial inheritance? In the bright ideas which he tried to exploit? A lucky combination of an able man with the right idea in the right place at the right time can—as in the case of men such as Ford—lead to an explosive growth of an individual property. We must regard society from the point of view of property ownership as subject to a series of random strokes of good and bad luck, upsetting continuously the existing pattern of ownership. But at the same time there are at work the systematic economic forces of accumulation and the systematic biological and demographic forces of inheritance which are some of them tending to equalize and some of them to disequalize ownership. The striking inequalities which we observe in the real world are the result of the balance of these systematic forces working in a society subject to the random strokes of luck. That is all we can say until this most important field for research and enquiry has been cultivated much more extensively than has been the case up to the present.

We turn then to stage three of our enquiry into the factors which affect the distribution of the ownership of property, namely governmental policy of various kinds. Let us start by considering the effects of various forms of tax.

We have already considered the possibility of using a progressive income tax as part of the machinery of the Welfare State to tax the rich in order to raise funds to subsidize the poor, and we have already noted the fact that progressive income tax of this kind may have adverse effects upon incentives to work, enterprise, and save. Such taxation will also have some effect as an equalizer of the distribution of the ownership of property. Since large properties are an important cause of high incomes, the subjection of high incomes to highly progressive taxation will reduce the ability to save of the owners of large properties more than it will reduce the ability to save of the owners of small properties. This will help the small properties to grow at a higher rate relatively to that of the large properties. This tendency will be still more marked in so far as the progressive income tax discriminates against unearned incomes and in favour of earned incomes. For a tax on incomes from property as contrasted with a tax on incomes from work is a more direct imposition on the owners of large properties as such.

But different properties may earn different incomes according to the form in which they are invested—cash earns nothing; short-dated gilt-edged securities a very small yield; and so on until one comes to the high average yields from risky and enterprising ventures. An annual tax of a progressive character which is based not on the level of total income nor even on the level of unearned income, but upon the value of the total property owned by the taxpayer is the tax which would most directly militate against large properties with the least adverse effects upon incentives to take risks and enterprise with one's capital. This tax like all progressive direct taxes is bound to reduce the level of private savings; it reduces the ability to accumulate capital by the richest citizens who are the most able to save.

Indeed, the essential argument in favour of these taxes which we are at present examining is that they will reduce the net savings and so the net capital accumulation of the largest property owners. If, because savings tend to fall below the optimum level (see p. 23 above), it is desired to maintain the level of total savings and at the same time to discourage the accumulation of the largest properties, it is essential to combine these progressive tax measures with other measures which will stimulate the savings of the small property owners and/or which will raise the public savings (the budget surplus) of the government itself. We will return to these alternative sources of savings in due course.

But while all forms of progressive taxation are likely to reduce private savings, we may legitimately ask which of these various measures of progressive tax will achieve a given reduction in the rate of growth of the largest properties with the minimum adverse effects on other economic incentives— namely the incentives to work and to take risks. All these forms of progressive taxation may well have some adverse effects upon incentives to work and risk as well as upon the level of savings. For one of the motives to work and risk is to achieve the large income which enables one to accumulate a large property for one's own enjoyment and to bequeath to one's children; and tax arrangements which beyond a point make it very difficult to accumulate property may blunt incentives to make the additional effort to earn the means for further accumulation. But it is probable that a progressive tax on unearned incomes will have less effect in reducing the incentive to earn than will a similar tax on earned incomes; and it is probable that an annual tax assessed on capital wealth (whether it be invested in secure or risky forms) will have less adverse effect upon enterprise than one based on unearned income (which is the fruit of risky rather than of secure investments). The case for an annual tax on capital wealth is thus a strong one. Its disadvantage is the serious extra administrative task of assessing persons' capital wealth as well as their annual incomes; but, as we shall see below, there are other desirable policies which may depend upon the assessment of individuals' capital wealth.

There is a second type of fiscal attack on the maldistribution of property—namely death duties. Can one find a system of tax which reduces very little the ability or incentive of the large property owner to work, enterprise, and accumulate during his life time, but which gives him a high incentive to distribute his property widely among those with small properties at his death?

If death duties are to be used seriously as an instrument for the equalization of properties, it is essential that gifts *inter vivos* should be taxed in the same way as bequests at death. Otherwise, as in the United Kingdom at present, the whole operation becomes farcical. Any rich property owner, in the absence of a similar tax on gifts *inter vivos*, can avoid any death-duty obstacle to the concentration of his own wealth into the possession of a single wealthy heir by transferring the greater part of his property as a gift during his life time. Treating gifts *inter vivos* in the same way as bequests at death raises administrative problems which it is essential to face if a serious effort is to be made by fiscal means to redistribute properties.

Let us consider four possible principles upon which death duties and taxes on gifts *inter vivos* might be assessed.

(i) First, there is the principle of the United Kingdom Estate duty according to which a duty is assessed at a progressive rate which rises according to the size of the total estate. In the United Kingdom at present the rate of duty starts at 1 per cent on estates of £5,000 and rises by gradual increments to 80 per cent on estates of over £1,000,000. A progressive estate duty of this kind (provided that it is accompanied by similar taxation of gifts *inter vivos*) must, of course, exercise a strong equalizing tendency on the distribution of property as it taxes at progressively higher rates the large properties as they pass at death. But it does nothing to induce the rich property owner to distribute his property on his death more widely among a number of beneficiaries.

(ii) The second possible principle would be to tax estates passing at death and gifts *inter vivos* according to the size of the individual bequest. Thus an estate of £1,000,000 bequeathed to a single heir might be taxed at 80 per cent; but if it were left in 100 bequests of £10,000 each, each bequest might be taxed only at 6 per cent.[1] This principle would certainly improve the incentive to split up large properties at death. But it would not encourage the large property owners in choosing his numerous beneficiaries to give preference to those who were not already the owners of large properties.

[1] This is the present rate of United Kingdom duty on estates of £10,000.

If a large number of rich men split up their estates among a large number of rich children, little is gained as compared with the situation in which each rich man leaves the whole of his estate to one rich child.

(iii) A third principle would be to tax each individual gift or bequest not solely according to the size of the individual gift or bequest but also according to the existing wealth of the beneficiary. Thus a higher rate of duty would be paid according to the total property which the beneficiary would possess when the gift or legacy was added to his existing wealth.[1] This principle would give a strong incentive to large property owners not only to split their properties into many parts, but also to bequeath these parts to persons who were already the owners of only small properties.

This principle (iii) has an added advantage over the previous principle (ii). If principle (ii) is adopted, it is possible to avoid duty by making successive gifts to the same person, unless special provisions are introduced to remove this possibility. Thus under principle (ii) if A wishes to pass £1,000,000 on to B, he will pay, say, 80 per cent in tax if he passes his fortune in one single lump. But if he passes on by gift one £500,000 to B this year and the other £500,000 to B some years later, he will pay only the reduced rate of duty appropriate to the smaller gift on each of the two halves of his fortune. This possibility is very much reduced by the application of principle (iii). If the beneficiary B has had his fortune increased in one year by £500,000, the rate of tax payable on the second £500,000 will be greatly increased.

Principle (iii) does, however, require that the value of the existing capital wealth of any beneficiary should be assesssed, as well as the value of the gift or bequest itself, in order that the tax liability should be assessed. If an annual tax on capital wealth were itself introduced, this would itself provide an assessment of individual's capital wealth which would be available for the assessment of the duty payable on gifts and bequests under principle (iii).

[1] An actual scale of duty which might be used is expounded in Appendix III (pp. 88-90 below).

(iv) With the fourth principle every gift or legacy received by any one individual would be recorded in a register against his name for tax purposes. He would then be taxed when he received any gift or bequest neither according to the size of that gift or bequest nor according to the size of his total property at the time of the receipt of that gift or bequest, but according to the size of the total amount which he had received over the whole of his life by way of gift or inheritance. The rate of tax would be on a progressive scale according to the total of gifts or bequests recorded against his name in the tax register.

The rich propery owner would now have every incentive to pass on his property in small parcels to persons who had up to date received little by way of gift or inheritance. This system should serve to diffuse property ownership with the minimum adverse effects upon incentives to earn, enterprise, save, and accumulate property. The testator or donor could avoid tax on handing on his property by leaving a moderate amount to each of a number of persons who had not yet received much by way of gift and inheritance. And, unlike principle (iii), no prospective heir would be discouraged from accumulating a property of his own by his own efforts: the duty which he would have to pay on the receipt of any subsequent gift or bequest would not be higher because he had already enriched himself by his own efforts. It would only be higher if he had already been enriched by the receipt of property from someone else.

Principle (iv) would thus probably be superior to principle (iii) in its effects on incentives to work, risk, and accumulate. Moreover, with principle (iv) unlike principle (iii) there would be no incentive at all to hand over one's property in small successive doses to any one heir, because the tax payable would be progressive according to the total amount received by gift or inheritance regardless of the timing and size of each individual gift or bequest. On the other hand principle (iii) would have a more equalizing effect than principle (iv), since it would discourage the passing on of property to rich men whether the source of their riches was their own effort or not.

From the administrative point of view principle (iv) is probably basically simpler than principle (iii). Both principles require the assessment of the value of each gift or bequest when it is made; but principle (iv), unlike principle (iii), does not require the assessment of the beneficiary's existing wealth as well. All that it requires is the assessment and recording of the receipt of each separate gift or bequest. If, however, all individuals' properties were already being regularly assessed for the purpose of an annual tax on capital wealth, principle (iii) might well be the simpler from an administrative point of view; for the assessment of a beneficiary's existing property would already be available for the tax on capital wealth and no record of previous gifts or bequests would be needed.

Principles (ii), (iii), and (iv) all raise a problem in the case of discretionary trusts. For if property is left in such a way that the trustees are able to exercise a discretion at some time in the future as to who should be the actual beneficiary from the property, it is not possible to assess the size of the individual bequests enjoyed by particular beneficiaries at the time of the passing of the property from its previous owner. There are three possible lines of attack on this problem. The first would be to legislate in such a way as to restrict considerably the possibilities of setting up such trusts. The second would be to ensure that such properties were not taxed at the time of the setting up of the trust, but were taxed as and when the funds were in fact used to enrich individual beneficiaries. The third would be to name some rather high, but arbitrary fixed rate of duty which the tax authorities could levy on such trust funds at the time when they were set up and which would exempt such funds from further tax when they were actually used to the benefits of particular individuals.[1]

So much for the progressive taxation of income or wealth. Such fiscal measures are not, however, the only policy measures which may substantially affect the distribution of the owner-

[1] Some other and perhaps lower fixed rate of duty might be set for all charitable gifts and bequests.

ship of property. Arrangements which encourage the accumulation of property by those with little property are certainly as important as those which discourage further accumulation or encourage dispersal of their fortunes by large property owners. Such arrangements might include: the encouragement of financial intermediaries in which small savings can be pooled for investment in high-earning risk-bearing securities; measures to promote employee share schemes whereby workers can gain a property interest in business firms; and measures whereby municipally built houses can be bought on the instalment principle by their occupants.

We have already noted (pp. 30-32 above) the extreme importance of education as a form of investment which affects earning power. Future developments of educational policy could have a profound effect upon the distribution of earning power and so indirectly, through the power to accumulate, upon the distribution of property. We have already explained how in the past the spread of public elementary education in the developed countries has almost certainly been an important equalizing factor. It has in essence been an investment of capital with a high return, financed out of general taxation for the benefit of every citizen; indeed in countries like the United Kingdom where the rich, in addition to contributing through taxation to the general system of public education, have invested their own funds in their own childrens' education in private schools, public education financed from general taxation has represented an educational investment in the children of the poor.

There is undoubtedly great scope for educational developments which will have further equalizing effects of the same kind. We are becoming aware[1] how greatly within the State system of education itself environmental factors of one kind or another enable the children of the relatively rich to gain more than the children of the poor from such education. It may be that steps can be taken to counteract these forces. Moreover many educational developments, such as the raising

[1] See, for example, Brian Jackson and Dennis Marsden *Education and the Working Class* and J. W. B. Douglas *The Home and the School*.

of the minimum school-leaving age or the improvement (through the reduction in the size of classes) of the education which is common to all, will expand the equalizing forces which have been so prominent in the past.

But the picture is less certain when one considers possible educational developments in higher education at Universities and similar institutions. There is, of course, one extremely important way in which the expansion of higher education is likely to exercise an equalizing influence. Highly trained persons command a higher wage than do the untrained and the unskilled; the transformation of the relatively untrained into the highly trained through an expanded programme of higher education will decrease the supply of the former and increase the supply of the latter type of worker; the low wages of the unskilled should thus be raised relatively to the high wages of the trained as there are fewer untrained and more trained persons seeking employment in the labour market.

But, on the other hand, there are two reasons for believing that future developments of higher education may be less equalizing than were the earlier educational developments. Indeed they might conceivably in the end turn out to be positively disequalizing in their effects upon ability to earn and to accumulate property.

The first of the marked differences between elementary and higher education is in the division of the costs of such education between the State and the students or their families. None of the cost of elementary education takes the form of earnings foregone; the young boys and girls would not nowadays be in the factories if they were not in the schools. But for higher education earnings foregone make up a very large part, indeed the greater part,[1] of the cost. Though the State provides free of charge the actual educational services and even if it pays in addition some modest maintenance allowances to students, there is a very substantial cost borne by the student or his family in earnings foregone. Such a cost can be more easily met by the rich than by the poor parent. Higher education still involves the investment of private property in the

[1] See Theodore W. Schultz *op. cit.*, table on p. 29.

60

student; and the children of poor parents may be discouraged from it by the desire to start earning at an early date.

But the second difference between elementary and higher education is probably much more important. Even though there is a great expansion in the numbers who receive higher education, it will remain selective; and the basis of selection will be more and more the able boy or girl rather than the son or daughter of wealthy parents. This means increased equality of opportunity. But equality of opportunity is not the same thing as equality of outcome. Indeed, greater equality of opportunity could in the long-run mean less, and not greater, equality of wealth. Of course, as between two boys of equal ability, if the son of the poor man is given the same opportunity as the son of the rich man, their ultimate earnings will be equalized. Equality of opportunity does lead to equality of result between those with equal ability. But not all have the same ability and the whole object of selection for higher education will be to select those who are innately able to enjoy the advantages of higher education.

When all have the same access to higher education, it will be the innately able who will succeed. Innate ability will receive the high earnings, accumulate property, and rise in the property scale. This rise of the meritocracy[1] will cause there to be a closer association between ability, earning power, and property at the top of the scale and between lack of ability, low earning power, and small property at the bottom of the scale. The ultimate inequalities in the ownership of property could be greater than before.

The outcome will depend very much upon the educational principle which is adopted. Here there is a possibility of a conflict between 'efficiency' and 'distributional' considerations in educational policy which is not always fully appreciated. Let us suppose that there is a certain additional amount of money which is going to be spent on education. How should it be spent? On reducing the size of classes in the primary schools? On raising the school-leaving age for all children? On increasing the period at the University for the ablest

[1] See Michael Young, *The Rise of the Meritocracy.*

students? On enabling a number of less able students to go to the University?

Now there are many ends to be attained through education other than economic ends. I do not wish to depreciate these ends and in the ultimate choice they will no doubt play an important role in the formation of educational policy. But I do not intend to discuss them on this occasion simply because I want to concentrate attention on the economic effects of educational expenditures. One economic principle for the use of resources in education would be to devote them to those uses which would increase most the productivity and future earning power of the students concerned. I will call this the 'efficiency' principle. Another economic principle would be to use the available resources in education in such a way as to equalize the future earning power of different students. I will call this the 'distributional' principle. Taken to its logical extreme the 'distributional' principle would mean concentrating educational effort and training facilities on the dullards to the neglect of the bright students until the educational advantages of the former just made up for the greater inborn abilities of the latter in the future competition for jobs.

But what would the 'efficiency' principle involve? It is very probable that in the past there was little or no conflict between the 'efficiency' and the 'distributional' principle—universal elementary education was needed on both tickets. But now that this stage in education is virtually complete, will such harmony reign in the future? I do not know; but it would be of great importance if it could be discovered whether, given the present stage of educational development, further expenditure on simple improvements in the basic education of all (for example, smaller classes in primary schools, a higher minimum school-leaving age), or a concentration of expenditure on a few able men and women (for example, more expensive laboratory facilities in the Universities and longer periods of postgraduate work for the ablest technicians) would in fact increase the national product most. It is possible that automation itself may mean that production would be most effectively promoted by the most profound training of a few technicians rather than by the general training of the many. There is a crying need for yet more research into these matters. It may be that the most efficient educational developments will also tend to equalize earning ability and so indirectly property ownership. But one would be betraying one's calling to hold this view without enquiry simply because it is a comfortable view to hold.

I come now to the controversial subject of public policies which might be adopted to influence differential fertility among different sections of society. There is an old standing conflict of view here. The radical left-winger in politics lays great stress on the importance of environment in determining a citizen's achievement in social life. The conservative right-winger lays great stress on the importance of inherited genetical ability in determining performance. It is fashionable today among students of society who wish to improve affairs to lay all the emphasis on improvements of one kind or another in environmental conditions in sharp contrast to the excesses of the early conservative Social Darwinists who saw the amelioration of society largely in terms of promoting the breeding of the successful rich and of discouraging the breeding of the unsuccessful poor.

I regard this dichotomy as unfortunate and unnecessary. As a radical in politics, but a believer in Eugenics I would like to explain briefly my views on this matter because it is very relevant to the problem of the distribution of the ownership of property which we are discussing. I am as impressed as any environmentalist by the importance of social reform to enable all citizens to develop in the best way their innate capacities both of intelligence and of character. But the greater is the success of radical environmental policies of this kind, the greater probably are both the need for and the possibility of a eugenic policy. For there is likely to be some truth in the old eugenic view that as society makes it easier for all—whatever may be their innate characteristics—to survive and to flourish, so there is a greater need for a conscious humane policy, other than the cruelties of the laissez-faire competitive struggle,

63

to restrain the reproduction of those who are innately ill-fitted ·
to make their way in society.

But eugenic policies will at the same time be becoming not
only more necessary but also more possible. For consider
what will be happening as we environmentalist radicals (for
I insist on having it both ways and numbering myself among
them) increase the real opportunities for achievement in
education, reduce the inequalities in endowment in inherited
wealth and opportunity to earn, and so reorganize society
that both the private and public demands for goods and
services increasingly represent the real needs of private consumers and the desirable public ends of society. We shall be
moving to a state of affairs in which there are ever increasing
positive correlations (i) between wealth and innate ability to
earn and (ii) between ability to earn and ability to serve the
real needs of society. Measures which encourage some differential fertility in favour of those whose earnings are high will
become increasingly eugenic in their effect and will be less
and less open to criticism on other grounds.

What form might such measures take?

An undesirably high rate of population growth is nowadays
almost universal throughout the world and is certainly once
again a real threat in the United Kingdom. It is essential that
any change in differential fertility should be based upon a
substantial reduction in fertility at the lower end of the scale
rather than in a rise in fertility at the top end.

For the lower end of the scale I would advocate extensive
positive and open measures by the public health and welfare
services to bring the full choice of means for contraception
within everyone's reach and understanding—and particularly
within the reach and understanding of the 'problem families'.
It is still true in the United Kingdom that the rich, successful,
and intelligent have readier access to contraceptive methods
than the poor, unsuccessful, and unintelligent.

For the top end of the scale I would suggest that in due
course tax arrangements might be recast so as to make it
taxwise more advantageous for those with high earned incomes
to have children. This can be done just as well by increasing

the tax burden on the childless rich as it can by decreasing the tax burden on the high earners who have the larger families. I am not advocating anything which reduces the taxation of the rich relatively to the poor, but something which reduces the taxation of the high earners with children as contrasted with the childless rich. There is no reason why at the higher end of the scale of incomes, the tax on earned incomes should not differentiate more than it does at present in favour of the larger families. Another suitable measure would be the removal of the means test for the public maintenance of children in higher education so that the bringing up of a family was a smaller cost than it is at present to the richer parents.

Let me remove certain possible misconceptions. In the moderate eugenic policy which I have advocated there is no where any element of compulsion. Any parents would be free to have whatever sized family they choose. There is also no suggestion that the ability to earn is the only desirable quality, but merely that, particularly in a society which had been reformed environmentally, ability to earn is one of the desirable sets of qualities which should be encouraged. Even within the set of qualities which gave ability to earn there is, of course, an enormous variety: musical ability, mathematical ability, general intelligence, qualities of leadership, physical abilities of various kinds, and so on and so on. Above all versatility and variety would be encouraged. This is a quite different matter from the encouragement of one very specialized and particular set of characteristics.

Finally let me remind you of the relevanace of all this to the main theme of these lectures. I would be the last person to advocate policy measures to discourage the fertility of the poor or to promote the fertility of the rich simply in order to equalize the ownership of property—by splitting the large fortunes among many children and the small fortunes among few. But if such policy measures are desirable on other grounds —and I believe that as we reform society environmentally they will become increasingly desirable on eugenic grounds—they should be doubly welcome because they could incidentally make a substantial contribution to our problem of redistributing property ownership more equally.

VI

A Socialist State

Let us turn now to the Social Ownership of Property as an alternative means for combining an efficient level of the real wage rate with an equitable distribution of income. Suppose that by the wave of some alternative magic wand—and we will later examine the nature of this wand—the ownership of all property were transferred from private individuals to the State. The real wage rate is set at the level which enables it to be used exclusively as an 'efficiency' guide for the use of labour. If this 'efficiency' level is a low one, then a large part of the national income accrues as profits on capital of all kinds. But these profits now go to the State, which could use them to pay out an equal social dividend to every citizen. In one basic respect this system is the same as a system in which property is privately owned but is owned in equal amounts by every citizen. In both cases income from property is equally divided between all citizens.

In one important respect the social ownership of property has an important advantage over the equal distribution of private ownership. In the both cases, in the interests of preventing total savings from falling below the optimum level (see p. 23 above), private savings may need to be supplemented by public savings, particularly since with a more equal distribution of income from property there will remain no very large private incomes from property out of which high personal savings might have been made. In both cases the promotion of public savings through a budget surplus may be necessary. In the case in which property is in private ownership the achievement of the budget surplus will require increased tax revenue; and the rise in rates of taxation may have unfortunate effects on economic incentives. In the case of the social ownership of property, on the other hand, all income from property accrues to the State. The State can, therefore, generate a given level of public savings through the budget with a lower level of tax rates and therefore with less adverse effects on efficiency in the case of State ownership of property, than in the case of equalized private ownership of property.

At first sight it might appear that if all property were owned by the State, then all industrial activities would have to be managed in socialised concerns, so that the price mechanism would no longer be working in a free-enterprise competitive economy. This would not essentially alter our present argument. In a modern centrally planned and fully socialized economy it is increasingly difficult (because of the increasing complexity of relationships between different industries) to conduct affairs efficiently without using the mechanism of prices of various inputs and outputs as measures of their relative scarcities. Thus in a centrally planned and fully socialized economy with an automated technique of production the level of the real wage rate which will act as the efficient guide for the use of labour may be very low. In this case the profits of state enterprises will be high. But these profits will be available to the State to use in any way which the State decides to be equitable.

But in fact there is no one-to-one relationship between the amount of real property which is directly managed by the State (as in the case of a socialized industry) and the amount of the economy's total real wealth which is in the unencumbered possession of the State. The two things may differ because of the existence of a national debt. There are in fact two quite distinct measures of the degree of socialist ownership of property, which we may express as

$$\frac{K_s}{K} \quad \text{and} \quad \frac{K_s - D}{K}$$

where K is the value of the total real property of the community (the value of all the land, buildings, plant, machinery, and stocks of goods in the community), K_s is the part of this total which is directly managed by the State (the land, buildings, plant, machinery, and stocks of goods used in the provision of public services or in socialized industries), and D is the value of the national debt owed by the State and other public authorities to the private sector of the economy. In the United Kingdom at the present time K is some £50,000 million, K_s £21,000 million and D £28,000 million[1] so that

$$\frac{K_s}{K} = 42\% \quad \text{and} \quad \frac{K_s - D}{K} = -14\%.$$

While some 42 per cent of the real property of the community is in the management-ownership of the State or other public authorities, the value of the total amount of property owned privately is actually greater than the value of the total real property of the community, because the national debt is greater than the real property owned by the State or other public authorities.[2]

For our present purpose we are interested in the measure $\frac{K_s - D}{K}$. We are interested, that is to say, in the ultimate destination of income from property and not in the immediate control over real property. In the United Kingdom at present $\frac{K_s - D}{K}$ is a negative quantity; we are dealing with a society in which, far from the State receiving a net income from

---

[1] I am indebted to Mr. J. R. S. Revell of the Department of Applied Economics in the University of Cambridge for these figures.

[2] At the other extreme it is possible to conceive of a state of affairs in which $\frac{K_s}{K}$ is practically zero but $\frac{K_s - D}{K}$ is practically $+100\%$. This would be the case if practically no real property were in the management-ownership of the State ($K_s = 0$), if private entrepreneurs managed and ran for competitive profit practically all the real property of the community, and if these private businesses were directly or indirectly financed to a very large extent by loans from the State (D is a large negative figure). The State would ultimately own most property; but this would take the form of the opposite of a national debt, namely a large indebtedness of private persons to the State. The State's loans might be made to individuals, to business companies, or to investment trusts which held shares in business. Business would be managed on a competitive free enterprise basis, but ultimate ownership of much property would be in the hands of the State.

property for use as it seems equitable, private property owners own more property than the total real property of the community and the State is a net debtor to the private sector. As far as the management of real property is concerned we live in a semi-Socialist State; but as far as the net ownership of property is concerned we live, not in a semi-Socialist State, but in an anti-Socialist State.

Suppose, however, that, by a wave of our present magic wand, this position could be reversed and a large part of private property became public property so that $\dfrac{K_s - D}{K}$ was transformed from a negative figure to a large positive fraction. It is, of course, merely a question of degree how far this should go. But the larger is $\dfrac{K_s - D}{K}$, the larger will be the State's income from productive capital (K_s) or the smaller will be the State's current expenditure on interest on the national debt (D). What advantages or disadvantages would this change have?[1] The Socialization of the ownership of property will give the State a larger net income from property and in consequence rates of taxation can be reduced or larger social-security payments can be made to the poorer members of society without any reduction in other forms of State expenditure. The *gross* incomes of the private sector are lower because less interest is paid on the national debt or less profit is received on property now transferred to the State; but *net* incomes of the private sector are unchanged because taxation is lower or social-security benefits are higher. There is an improvement in economic incentives and/or in the distribution of income because of the lower rates of tax and/or the equitable social benefits. At the same time, since private net incomes are the same, but private properties are smaller, there is likely to be an improvement in the incentives for private savings.

---

[1] For a fuller discussion of this point see J. E. Meade 'Is the National Debt a Burden?' and 'Is the National Debt a Burden? A Correction', *Oxford Economic Papers*, June 1958 and February 1959.

Is there then nothing to be said in favour of private property? If the foregoing argument contained the whole of the truth, then the greater the ratio $\dfrac{K_s - D}{K}$ the better for society. Best of all would be the absence of all private property; the state would be able to go to the utmost in the reduction of tax and/or in the increase of social benefits and thus achieve the maximum improvements in incentives and/or in the equitable distribution of income. But, alas, as is so often the case in this wicked world there is much to be said on both sides of the question. Private property does have advantages. A man with the same net income of £1,000 without any property (situation I) and with £10,000 of property (situation II) is better off in situation II than in situation I. The property itself gives him security and independence. If this were the whole of the story, the State could always improve matters by printing and handing out to every citizen another £1,000,000 of national debt and raising each citizen's taxes to the extent necessary to cover the interest on £1,000,000 of debt. Each citizen would have the same net income as before and each would be a millionaire into the bargain. Where is the snag? Simply that the rate of tax of 19s 11¾d. in the £[1] (or whatever would be necessary to meet the gigantic bill for interest on the debt) would kill all economic incentives. We would all sit back and do nothing intending to live on our ample capital, and economic life would grind to a standstill.

Thus if we started from a position with no private property, as the amount of private property rose (i.e. as $\dfrac{K_s - D}{K}$ fell) (i) tax incentives would worsen but (ii) the security and independence gained from property ownership would rise. As we proceeded the extra loss from (i) would become more and more acute and the extra gain from (ii) less and less important. Somewhere there is an optimum point though I am afraid that I cannot tell you where it is. Indeed, I am not sure that I can even define it rigorously.

[1] For the sake of the uninstructed may I explain that this is a British way of saying 99·9 per cent.

But I have a hunch that it would be better if the index $\dfrac{K_s - D}{K}$ (now so low that it is highly negative) were substantially raised in the United Kingdom, particularly if the property which did remain in private ownership could simultaneously be much more equally distributed. In my view what we need is a combination of measures for some socialisation of net property ownership and for a more equal distribution of the property which is privately owned.

But what is the nature of our socialist magic wand? How can some socialization of the net ownership of property be achieved? It would be possible to devise a once-for-all capital levy which transferred some slice of property from each private property owner to the State. This direct method is, I fear, open to serious objection. It would in any case be administratively difficult. But apart from that we are faced with the following dilemma. For it to be a success it must be accepted as a once-for-all measure which will not be repeated; otherwise the fear of a repetition would kill all future incentives to accumulate capital. But for it to be both successful and accepted as being unlikely to be repeated, it must be on a very large scale; it must be believed that it will not be repeated simply because enough transfer to the State has already been achieved. But if it is on a very large scale, the administrative and political, to say nothing of the economic and financial, difficulties of the operation will be very great indeed.

Much more practicable is to devise a suitable budgetary policy which will result in a continuing substantial annual budget surplus which, year by year, can be used for the redemption of the national debt (so that D falls) or for investment in State-controlled income-earning assets (so that K_s rises). For this purpose one needs to find a form of tax by which considerable additional revenue may be raised with the minimum adverse effects upon the incentives to work and enterprise. But it does not matter for our present purpose if the tax does discourage private savings. Our whole purpose is to use the tax to increase public savings through the budget; even if it does this wholly at the expense of private savings, total savings would not thereby be reduced. If the tax is paid only partially out of private savings, but is used wholly to add to public savings, there will be some net increase in total savings. As we have already argued (pp. 53–54 above), a progressive annual tax assessed on the capital value of individual properties would probably have minimal adverse effects upon incentives to work and enterprise, though it would discourage the accumulation of the largest private properties. It would seem, therefore, to be a suitable additional tax for the increased socialisation of net property ownership.

In advocating in this way the old-fashioned policy of generating a budget surplus in order to redeem national debt, I am not forgetting the overriding importance of using financial policy for the maintenance of full employment and the promotion of economic growth. When the economy is threatened with stagnation because effective demand is not growing sufficiently to maintain a full pressure upon the available real resources of the community, expenditure on goods and services both for consumption and for investment should be stimulated by a monetary policy (which eases the terms on which funds can be borrowed for expenditure) and by a tax policy (which increases the funds available for, and the incentive for, expenditures on goods and services.) What is needed is short-run flexibility of monetary and tax policies to preserve the desired level of effective demand in the interests of full employment and economic expansion. Over the long-run average of years this flexible short-run monetary and budgetary policy, while it is successful in controlling total demand so as to maintain the full employment of resources, may fail in either of two other ways. (i) It may fail to maintain the 'optimum level of savings' which in the ultimate analysis means a failure to ensure that a sufficiently large part of the desired total expenditure takes the form of expenditure on new capital goods for investment for the benefit of future consumers, too large a part being devoted to expenditure on current consumption. (ii) It may, secondly, fail to maintain a sufficiently high surplus of tax revenue over current budgetary expenditure to ensure that there is the desired rate of gradual socialization of property ownership.

To remedy failures (i) or (ii) it is not desirable to abandon the short-run flexibilities of monetary and budgetary policies designed to maintain full employment, but to alter the structure of financial policies so that the outcome of these flexible monetary and budgetary policies over the average of the years does not display either of these two undesirable weaknesses. Thus to remedy failure (i), measures to promote expenditure on investment (e.g. an easier monetary policy or special tax remissions on investment expenditures) may be combined with measures to restrict consumption expenditures (e.g. higher rates of tax on spendable incomes.) Or to remedy failure (ii) measures may be taken to increase the total of tax revenue without any adverse restriction of total private expenditure on goods and services; for example, rates of tax might be raised in the case of duties which are likely to be paid out of past savings rather than out of current expenditures on consumption or capital goods (such as death duties or an annual tax on wealth) and any minor adverse effects of these tax increases in reducing expenditures might be offset by much smaller tax reductions in the case of duties which are likely to have been paid mainly out of reduced expenditures (such as taxes on spendable incomes).

In fact the State has many different financial weapons: monetary policy which can affect total expenditure and in particular expenditure on new capital goods without any direct effect upon the budgetary surplus; some taxes which will discourage above all expenditure on consumption; other taxes which discourage above all investment expenditures on capital goods; yet other taxes which raise revenue primarily from property already accumulated and discourage neither consumption nor investment very substantially; and many forms of subsidy and tax remission which will affect either consumption or investment expenditures. Short-run changes in monetary and budgetary policies should continuously be made to maintain full employment. But structural changes in the balance between monetary policy and various forms of

73

tax and subsidy can also be made. By such structural changes short-run adjustments of monetary and tax policies for the maintenance of full employment can be made compatible with long-run averages over the years of an optimum level of total savings and of an optimum budget surplus by means of which there is the desired gradual socialization of property ownership.

VII

Conclusion

The problem discussed in the preceding chapters has been presented in its most acute form in terms of the future of our economy if automation reduces markedly the importance in productive processes of men relative to that of machines. We have argued that to combine efficiency in the use of resources with equity in the distribution of income would in that case cry out for measures to equalize the distribution of the owner-ship of private property and to increase the net amount of property which was in social ownership. But the problem is not simply a hypothetical one of the future. Private property is at present greatly inflated by the national debt, and is very unequally distributed. With a real wage rate that acted as an 'efficient' price, property income (without any further auto-mation) is already a very important element of total income. The combination of efficiency-in-use with equity-in-distribution already calls in the United Kingdom for measures for the equalization and the socialization of property ownership. These measures are needed, for the most part, to supplement rather than to replace the existing Welfare-State policies.

The sort of measures which might be appropriate for these purposes are:

(1) a radical reform of the death duties which turned them into a progressive tax dependent upon the total amount which each beneficiary had received up to date by way of gift or inheritance;

(2) the extension of the reformed death duties to cover gifts *inter vivos*;

(3) the generation of a substantial budget surplus for the

75

redemption of the national debt or for investment in other appropriate forms of public property by means of a progressive annual tax assessed on capital wealth;

(4) the encouragement of institutional forms (such as profit-sharing schemes, the instalment purchase of municipal houses by their tenants, and the development of suitable investment trusts) which would make easier and more profitable the accumulation of small properties;

(5) the development of educational policies which would equalize the chances of promotion in life for boys and girls of equal innate ability; and

(6) the reduction of the relative fertility of those with low earning capacity (i) by giving easy and equal opportunity to all citizens for acquiring and using contraceptives and (ii) by increasing the tax burden of the childless relatively to those with children within the high earned-income brackets.

The adoption of this six point programme could greatly change the social structure of the United Kingdom. But there remains one major difficulty in its implementation which has not so far been mentioned. The world is made up of a number of separate national states with ever increasing communication and movement between those which practice a free and liberal way of life. It might be difficult for one such nation alone to implement as fully as it would otherwise desire the sort of programme outlined above. No one perhaps can tell in advance for any one country how great would be the incentives for the able and enterprising to move from a country in which measures had been deliberately taken to damp down the accumulation of the biggest private properties to countries in which no or few such measures were in operation. Undoubtedly in some cases at least some moderation in the rate of reform would be necessary on these grounds. The main moral is a simple one. In this, as in so much of their economic and social policies, it is not necessary that all the liberal countries should adopt precisely the same policies. But it is desirable that they should keep very broadly in step in their general philosophy and practice of reform. Otherwise the only alternative might be the growth of illiberal national controls over international movements. The problem of the ownership of property is, in my view, one of great importance and of common concern throughout the free world.

The Distribution of Personal Incomes. The United Kingdom, 1959[1]

The figures given in Table 2 of the main text (p. 29) are to be regarded as rough indications of the order of magnitude of the problems involved in the United Kingdom rather than an exact representation of the actual situation. At that point of the argument in the main text we were neglecting the efforts of State action and in particular the effects of taxation, of social security benefits, of the State ownership of property, and of State indebtedness to the private sector (the national debt). In the absence of the State the distribution of the cost of the national product (i.e. of the net national income) between wages and salaries on the one hand and interest, profits, and rents on the other hand would coincide with the distribution of personal incomes between earned incomes and incomes from property. But the existence of the State breaks this one-to-one correspondence in many ways. For example, part of interest, profit, and rent (e.g. the profits of nationalized industries and the profits tax levied on companies' profits) will accrue directly as budgetary revenue to the State and will not appear in the figures of personal incomes. On the other hand, interest payable on the national debt is part of personal incomes, but is not part of the interest cost of the national product. Other transfer payments (e.g. social security benefits) are also part of personal incomes but not part of the factor cost of the national product. In the case of wages, employers' compulsory insurance contributions are part of the labour cost of the national product but will not appear in the statistics of personal wage earnings.

In the United Kingdom there is a special reason why the figures of personal incomes derived from the Income Tax returns will seriously

[1] I am indebted to Mr. J. R. S. Revell and Mr. A. Armstrong of the Department of Applied Economics of the University of Cambridge for the figures on which this Appendix is based.

underestimate personal incomes from property. They exclude capital gains. But the increase in the value of companies' shares which is due to the accumulation of undistributed profits represents in effect a personal income of the shareholders which has been saved for them by the companies themselves. Similarly, the interest and dividends received by the life funds of insurance companies enhances the capital value of the life assurance policies, though it does not appear in the statistics of the personal incomes of the owners of the life policies.

The figures in Table 5 give for 1959 the distribution of personal incomes declared for tax in the United Kingdom. The figures for the

Table 5. Personal Incomes (before deduction of tax) in the United Kingdom, 1959

Percentage of Total Population with Largest Personal incomes from all Sources	Percentage of Total Personal Incomes from all Sources (i)	Percentage of Personal Incomes from Property (p)	Percentage of Personal Incomes from Earnings (l)
1	9	47	6
5	21	66	17
10	31	73	27
Total Income £ million	15,391	1,184	14,207

p's and l's given in the two last columns of Table 5 are those used for the p's and l's in Table 2 of the main text. But the Inland Revenue figures in Table 5 show personal incomes from property (£1,184 m.) as only 7.1 per cent of total personal incomes (£15,391 m.). This value for the ratio $(1-q)$ is certainly a gross underestimate.

In the net national income as a whole for 1959 interest, profits, and rents made up 19.1 per cent of the total. In the gross national product for 1959 earned incomes are estimated as £15,966 m. and the remainder of the gross national product at £5,192 m. But to obtain the relevant figures for the net national product we must deduct a depreciation allowance of £1,904 m., £400 m. in respect of earned incomes and £1,504 m. in respect of other income. This gives property income after depreciation (£3,688 m.) as 19.1 per cent of total net national income after depreciation (£19,254 m.). This

19.1 per cent would, as we have seen, be the relevant value of our ratio $(1-q)$ in the absence of the State.

The figures for personal property incomes and earned incomes in Table 5 give £1,184 m. and £14,207 m. respectively. The figures for net property incomes and for wage incomes included in the net national product give £3,688 m. and £15,566 m. respectively. A rough reconciliation of these two sets of estimates is given in Table 6. From that Table it would seem that personal incomes from property in Table 5 may be underestimated by as much as £1,500 m. (£200 m. for certain deductions allowed by the Inland Revenue, £800 m. for underestimated profits net of depreciation, £200 m. for the incomes of life assurance funds, £300 m. for owner-occupied houses). If we add this figure to personal incomes from property and to total personal incomes in Table 5 we obtain a value of about 16 per cent for $(1-q)$.

Table 2 of the main text does no more than apply values for $(1-q)$ of 5, 15, and 25 per cent to the values for the p's and l's of Table 5.

Table 6. *Personal Incomes and the Net National Income Compared*

Property Incomes

		£m.
Personal Property Incomes as given in Table 5		1,184
Add	(i) Certain Deductions from Income allowed by the Inland Revenue	207
	(ii) Gross Undistributed Profits	2,321
	(iii) Direct Taxation paid by Companies (home and abroad)	1,169
	(iv) Additions to Life Assurance and Super-annuation Funds	236
	(v) Imputed Income from Owner-Occupied Houses	301
	(vi) Government Income from Property ..	618
Deduct	(i) National Debt Interest	− 915
	(ii) Depreciation on above Incomes	− 1,504
		3,617

Earned Incomes

Personal Earned Income as given in Table 5		14,207
Add	(i) Certain Deductions from Income allowed by the Inland Revenue	509
	(ii) Employers' National Insurance Contributions	990
	(iii) Income Received in Kind	179
	(iv) Capital Allowances for Self-Employed ..	98
	(v) Farmers' Incomes	534
Deduct	(i) Family Allowances and Pensions	− 639
	(ii) Depreciation on above Incomes	− 400
		15,478

The Accumulation of Personal Property

This Appendix provides greater precision for one or two of the relationships discussed on pp. 42-46 of the main text. Its main purpose, however, is to stress how much still remains to be done in this field and to stimulate others, better equipped than the author, to do it.

Assume that the amount which an individual saves and invests in new property (I) depends upon the size of his income (Y) and upon the size of his property (K). Since his savings are equal to what he adds to his property, we have

$$\frac{dK}{dt} \equiv I = I(Y, K) . \quad . \quad . \quad . \quad . \quad (1)$$

We suppose that his earned income (E) is equal to WL, where L is the amount of work which he chooses to do and W is the wage-rate which he can earn per unit of work done. His total income is composed of his earnings (E) and of his income from property (VK) where V is the rate of interest or profit which he can command on his property. It follows that

$$Y = E + VK = WL + VK \quad . \quad . \quad . \quad . \quad (2)$$

We may further assume that our individual's ability to earn and the rate of return on his property both depend partly upon the passage of time and partly upon the size of his property. In the case of the wage rate the labour market may be improving because of technical progress and capital accumulation in the economy as a whole, so that the wage he could earn would be rising even if his property were not growing. But in addition a larger property might give him a greater opportunity to earn, so that

$$W = W(K, t) \quad . \quad . \quad . \quad . \quad . \quad (3)$$

where t represents time. Similarly, the rate of profit on capital generally may be rising or falling over time in the economy as a

82

whole so that the return on his property will depend partly on the passage of time and partly on the size of his own property if at any one time large properties are able to earn higher returns than small properties. In this case,

$$V = V(K, t) \quad . \quad . \quad . \quad . \quad . \quad (4)$$

In the absence of birth or death or ageing and of governmental interventions (i.e. in stage one of our enquiring in the text on pp. 42-46) equations 1 to 4 give us a differential equation in K and t, which would show the growth pattern for our individual's property. By comparing the growth patterns of K' and K'' for two different individuals with different innate earnings abilities and different initial properties we could examine the movement of $\dfrac{K'}{K''}$ over time.

To do this we would have to have full information about the functions I, W, and V in equations 1, 3, and 4.

A more limited exercise is to ask whether, at the particular point of property accumulation reached by any one individual, the proportional rate of growth of his property $\left(k \equiv \dfrac{1}{K}\dfrac{dK}{dt}\right)$ is likely to be rising or falling. This may give us a clue as to which types of property will in fact be growing the more quickly. We can express equation 1 as $kK = I(Y, K)$; and by differentiation of this expression and of equations 2, 3, and 4 and on the assumption that L is constant we obtain:—

$$\frac{K}{k}\frac{dk}{dK} = -1 - E_{SK}$$

$$+ E_{SY}\left\{Q\left(E_{WK} + \frac{w}{k}\right) + (1-Q)\left(1 + E_{VK} + \frac{v}{k}\right)\right\} \quad . \quad (5)$$

where $E_{SK} = -\dfrac{K}{I}\dfrac{\partial I}{\partial K}$, $E_{SY} = \dfrac{Y}{I}\dfrac{\partial I}{\partial Y}$, $E_{WK} = \dfrac{K}{W}\dfrac{\partial W}{\partial K}$,

$E_{VK} = \dfrac{K}{V}\dfrac{\partial V}{\partial K}$, $w = \dfrac{1}{W}\dfrac{dW}{dt}$, $v = \dfrac{1}{V}\dfrac{dV}{dt}$, and $Q = \dfrac{WL}{Y}$, the proportion of earnings to total income. E_{SK} is an elasticity measure of the effect of an *increase* in property in *discouraging* savings. E_{SY} is an elasticity measure of the influence of a rise in income in encouraging savings. E_{WK} and E_{VK} are elasticity measures of the influence of increased property in increasing the ability to earn and the chance of getting a better return on property. w and v are the proportionate rates at which the wage rate and the rate of profit at which our citizen could sell his labour or invest his property would be changing in the market if his property were constant in size.

Whether at any particular point the growth rate of property (k) will be rising or falling as property (K) is being accumulated will depend upon whether

$$\frac{1 + E_{SK}}{E_{SY}} \lesseqgtr Q\left(E_{WK} + \frac{w}{k}\right) + (1 - Q)\left(1 + E_{VK} + \frac{v}{k}\right). \quad (6)$$

The growth rates w and v are external market phenomena. In a state of steady growth with a constant population, with a constant proportion of the national income going to wages, and with no relative shifts in the demand for different types of labour, w would be equal to the rate of growth of the total national income. In a state of steady growth v would be zero. But the importance of the parameter w in the inequality (6) would depend for any one individual very greatly upon the value of Q for him, i.e. upon the extent to which at that particular point of time in his accumulation process earnings were or were not of great importance in his total income. For a man with little property relatively to his earnings a high rate of increase of demand for labour in the market (w) would be an important factor raising the rate of accumulation of his property.

If we make some greatly simplified assumptions about the form of equations 1, 3, and 4 we can see how property would be accumulated over time. Let us assume that equation (1) is of the form

$$\frac{dK}{dt} = S(Y - \bar{Y}) - \theta K \quad \ldots \quad (7)$$

where S, $\bar{Y}$, and θ are constants. This would imply that if a man's property were zero, he would save a constant proportion (S) of the excess of his income over some basic subsistence level ($\bar{Y}$). His marginal propensity to save (S) would remain constant but his average propensity to save $\left(S - \frac{S\bar{Y}}{Y}\right)$ would rise and approach his marginal propensity to save (S) as his income (Y) increased. But we add the assumption that as his property grows this amount of savings is reduced by an amount θK, because the higher his property the less he needs to save.

Let us assume that in equations (3) and (4) both W and V are independent of K, that W grows through time at a constant proportional rate w, and that V remains constant, so that in place of equations (3) and (4) we have

$$W = W_0 e^{wt} \qquad \text{.} \quad \text{.} \quad \text{.} \quad \text{.} \quad \text{.} \quad \text{.} \quad (8)$$

$$\text{and } V = \text{constant} \quad \text{.} \quad \text{.} \quad \text{.} \quad \text{.} \quad \text{.} \quad (9)$$

From equations (2), (7), (8), and (9) we derive the differential equation

$$\frac{dK}{dt} = SW_0 Le^{wt} + (SV - \theta) K - S\hat{Y} \quad \text{.} \quad \text{.} \quad \text{.} \quad (10)$$

The solution of this equation gives

$$K = \frac{S\hat{Y}}{SV - \theta} + \frac{SW_0 L}{w + \theta - SV} e^{wt}$$

$$+ \frac{1}{V} \left(Y_0 - \hat{Y} - \frac{wW_0 L}{w + \theta - SV} \right) e^{(SV-\theta)t} \quad \text{.} \quad (11)$$

where $Y_0 = W_0 L + VK_0$.

The nature of the outcome of this process of accumulation will depend upon which of the two roots in (11) is the larger, w or $SV - \theta$. In our constant-population growing economy we can perhaps make a first approach to the relationship between w and $SV - \theta$ on the following lines. Consider a production function for the economy as a whole

$$Y^* = Y^* (K^*, t)$$

where the starred terms represent the aggregate sum of all the corresponding items for all the individual citizens. We have

$$\frac{1}{Y^*} \frac{dY^*}{dt} = \frac{\partial Y^*}{\partial K^*} \frac{\overline{dt}}{Y^*} + \frac{1}{Y^*} \frac{\partial Y^*}{\partial t}$$

We can write this as

$$y^* = S^* V + r \quad \text{.} \quad \text{.} \quad \text{.} \quad \text{.} \quad \text{.} \quad (12)$$

where y^* is the rate of growth of the total real national income, $V = \frac{\partial Y^*}{\partial K^*}$ is the rate of profit, S^* is the proportion of the total national income saved and invested, and $r \equiv \frac{1}{Y^*} \frac{\partial Y^*}{\partial t}$ is the rate of technical progress. If every individual has the same savings function as given in equation (7), then

$$S^* = \frac{SY^* - S\hat{Y}^* - \theta K^*}{Y^*}$$

where $\hat{Y}^* = \hat{Y}$ multiplied by the number of individual savers. It follows that

$$S - S^* = \frac{S\bar{Y}^* + \theta K^*}{Y^*} \quad . \quad . \quad . \quad . \quad (14)$$

Since $SV - \theta = S^*V + (S - S^*) V - \theta$,
we have from (12) and (14)

$$SV - \theta = y^* - r - \theta Q^* + SV \frac{\bar{Y}^*}{Y^*} \quad . \quad . \quad . \quad (15)$$

where $1 - Q^* = \dfrac{VK^*}{Y^*}$ is the proportion of the national income

paid in profits.

It follows from (15) that

$$w \gtreqless SV - \theta$$

according as

$$w - y^* + r + \theta Q^* \gtreqless SV \frac{\bar{Y}^*}{Y^*}$$

If the process of economic growth is such as to keep the proportion of the national income going to wages (Q^*) fairly constant, then w will be approximately equal to y^*. In this case

$$w > SV - \theta, \text{ if } r + \theta Q^* > SV \frac{\bar{Y}^*}{Y^*}$$

which is very likely to be the case.[1]

We are not, of course, yet building a reliable bridge between the theory of economic growth and the theory of the distribution of the ownership of property. For in the equations which refer to individuals, such as equation (11), we are simply assuming that w and V are constant. But the total amount saved by the community as a whole depends upon the aggregate of individual savings arising as each individual, starting from whatever situation he happens to be in, saves according to equation (10). But we have no right to assume w and V constant unless the aggregate savings which do so arise happen to provide such a level of total savings as do in fact (given the rate and form of technical progress) cause w and V to remain constant. We still need to incorporate into the general model of economic growth the savings which will result from our aggregate of individuals' behaviour and then see whether and, if so, along what path—starting from any arbitrarily given distribution of the ownership of property—the economy will approach a state of

[1] Suppose $S = \frac{1}{2}$, $V = 10$ per cent per annum, and $\dfrac{\bar{Y}^*}{Y^*} = \frac{1}{5}$, then if the rate of technical progress were more than 1 per cent per annum, w would be $> SV - \theta$ even if $\theta = 0$.

steady growth in which w and V will be constant and there will be a corresponding steady-state pattern for the distribution of the ownership of property. But until such a general model has been built we must content ourselves with the partial model of equation (11). If w and V were given and constant, then our individual's capital stock would behave as in equation (11).

If in equation (11) $w > SV - \theta$, then

$$\frac{1 - Q}{Q} \equiv \frac{KV}{WL} \longrightarrow \frac{SV}{w + \theta - SV} \text{ as } t \longrightarrow \infty.$$

The ratio of each individuals' unearned to his earned income will approach this value. Another way of putting this is to say that in each individuals' case the value of his property (K) will approach a given ratio $\left(\dfrac{S}{w + \theta - SV}\right)$ of his earnings. It follows that if there were two citizens 1 and 2 starting with different properties (K_0' and K_0'') and different earning powers ($W_0'L'$ and $W_0''L''$) but with the same savings function (S, θ, and $\bar{Y}$ the same for both) and the same market opportunities (w and V the same for both) they would end up with properties proportional to their earning powers, so that

$$\frac{K'}{K''} \longrightarrow \frac{W_0'L'}{W_0''L''} \text{ as } t \longrightarrow \infty.$$

If in equation (11), $w < SV - \theta$, then $\dfrac{1 - Q}{Q} \equiv \dfrac{KV}{WL}$ grows without limit. Income from property becomes an ever greater proportion of total income. But if we take again two individuals with different initial endowments of property and earning power but with the same savings functions and market opportunities, we find that

$$\frac{K'}{K''} \longrightarrow \frac{W_0'L' \dfrac{SV - \theta}{SV - \theta - w} + VK_0' - \bar{Y}}{W_0''L'' \dfrac{SV - \theta}{SV - \theta - w} + VK_0'' - \bar{Y}} \text{ as } t \longrightarrow \infty.$$

If $w = 0$, this means that the ratio between their properties will ultimately equal the ratio between the excesses of their initial incomes from work and property ($W_0L + VK_0$) over the basic subsistence level from which no saving is made ($\bar{Y}$). But if $SV - \theta > w > 0$, then it is still the initial excess of earned and unearned income over the subsistence level which will determine the outcome but with the initial earned income raised by the factor

$$\frac{SV - \theta}{SV - \theta - w}.$$

A Proposed Scale for a new Legacy and Gift Duty

If, as is discussed in the main text (p. 56), it were desired to make a new legacy and gift duty dependent upon the total wealth of the beneficiary, it would be necessary to devise a scale of progression for the duty which made the rate of duty dependent both upon the size of the beneficiary's existing property and also upon the size of the legacy or gift. It is suggested that the basic formula for the rate of tax (T) on the legacy or gift might be of the form $\dfrac{B + K}{B + C}$, where B is the value of the bequest, K is the value of the beneficiary's existing property before the receipt of the legacy or gift, and C is a constant. If $K \geqslant C$, the above formula for T would give a rate of duty $\geqslant 100$ per cent. Clearly one could not envisage a rate of duty above 100 per cent, so that one would have to set an upper limit to T. If one set this upper limit at 100 per cent, then C would represent the upper limit to which the value of an individual property could be raised by a legacy or gift. It is, however, proposed in this Appendix that an upper limit for T be set at 90 per cent, so that the rate of tax be $\dfrac{B + K}{B + C}$ or 90 per cent, whichever was the lower. It is also proposed in this Appendix that C be set at £100,000.

In order to avoid the administrative problems of taxing many small legacies and gifts, it is proposed that the first £1,000 of duty under the tax formula be remitted in all cases. The tax payable would thus be $TB - 1,000$ or nil, whichever were the greater.

Table 7 on page 89 shows the effect which this formula would have for various combinations of values of B and K. The figures against the lines D show the total duty payable under this formula, and those against the lines P show the total value of the property of the beneficiary after the receipt of the legacy or gift. The figures to

88

Table 7.—A Proposed Scale for Revised Duty on Gifts and Legacies. £000's

K, i.e. Property before Legacy or Gift

B, i.e. Gross Legacy or Gift		0	1	2	5	10	50	100	200	500	1000
1	D	0	0	0	0	0	0	0	0	0	0
	P	1	2	3	6	11	51	101	201	501	1001
2	D	0	0	0	0	0	0·02	0·8	0·8	0·8	0·8
	P	2	3	4	7	12	51·98	100·2	200·2	500·2	1000·2
5	D	0	0	0	0	0	1·6	3·5	3·5	3·5	3·5
	P	5	6	7	10	15	53·4	101·5	201·5	501·5	1001·5
10	D	0	0	0·1	0·36	0·82	4·5	8	8	8	8
	P	10	11	11·9	14·64	19·18	55·5	102	202	502	1002
50	D	15·7	16·0	16·3	17·3	19·0	32·3	44	44	44	44
	P	34·3	35·0	35·7	37·7	41·0	67·7	106	206	506	1006
100	D	49·0	49·5	50·0	51·5	54·0	74·0	89	89	89	89
	P	51	51·5	52·0	53·5	56·0	76·0	111	211	511	1011
200	D	132·3	133·0	133·7	135·7	139·0	165·7	179	179	179	179
	P	67·7	68·0	68·3	69·3	71·0	84·3	121	221	521	1021
500	D	415·7	416·5	417·3	419·8	424·0	449	449	449	449	449
	P	84·3	84·5	84·7	85·2	86·0	101	151	251	551	1051
1000	D	899	899	899	899	899	899	899	899	899	899
	P	101	102	104	106	111	151	201	301	601	1101

D shows the total Duty paid
P shows the value of the Property after receipt of legacy or gift and after payment of duty.

89

the North East of the heavy line are all cases in which no tax would be charged; those to the South West of the heavy broken line are all cases in which the fixed maximum rate of duty of 90 per cent would be payable. In the cases in between these lines an accurate valuation of existing properties as well as of legacies or gifts would be needed for the administration of the scheme.

Index

Accumulation of property, 41–6, 82–6
Advertisement, 12
Armstrong, A., 78
Assortative mating, 47
Automation, 25–6, 33, 35, 36, 40–1, 62–3, 75

Births, 47
Budgetary policy, 12, 22, 53, 71–4
Burt, Sir Cyril, 50

Capital levy, 71
Carter, C. O., 50
Contraception, 64, 76

Deaths, 47
Death duties, 54–8, 75, 88–90
Differential fertility, 47–8, 63–4, 76
Discretionary trusts, 58
Distribution of income and property in U.K., 27–30, 78–81
Douglas, J. W. B., 59

Earning power, 30–2, 48–9, 50–1, 59
Education, 30–2, 48–9, 59–62, 76
Efficiency, 11, 19–25
Estate duty, 55
Eugenics, 63–5
External economies and diseconomies, 12

Fisher, R. A., 51
Full employment, 12, 22, 36–7, 72–3

Genetic factors, 49–51
Gibson, John, 49–50
Gifts, *inter vivos*, 54, 55, 75

Inheritance, 47, 54–8
Intelligence, 49–50

Jackson, Brian, 59

Luddite activity, 37

Marginal product of labour, 24–6
Marriage, 47
Marsden, Dennis, 59
Mauritius, 14–19
Minimum wage, 35–7
Monetary policy, 12, 22, 72–3
Monopoly, 12
Myrdal, G., 43

National debt, 67–72, 75, 76, 78
National Economic Development Council, 12, 21

Obsolescence, 24
Optimum saving, 21–3, 53, 66, 72–4
Optimum time path, *see* Optimum saving
Ownership of property, 13, 38–9, 40–74 *passim*

Pasinetti, L., 41–2
Population, 14, 24, 64
Primary products, 13
Problem families, 64
Progressive taxation, 38, 52–4, 66–7, 69–70

Regression towards the mean, 50–1
Restrictive practices, 12, 37
Revell, J. R. S., 27, 68, 78

91

Savings function, 45–6, 82–7
Schultz, Theodore W., 30–2, 60
Social benefits, 66, 69–70
Social class, 49–50
Social Darwinists, 63
Social mobility, 49–50
Socialism, 66–74 *passim*
Stone, J. R. N., 45
Sugar, 14–17

Tea, 16
Trade Unions, 35–7

Unemployment, 36–7

Wage-rate, 13, 17, 23–6, 35–7
Wealth tax, 53, 54, 56, 58, 72
Welfare State, 38–9, 75

Young, Michael, 49–50, 61

J. E. MEADE

GEOMETRY OF INTERNATIONAL TRADE

In the course of his preparation of that work Professor Meade elaborated a geometrical technique to aid his own analysis of a number of the problems which he encountered. The present book, *A Geometry of International Trade*, is a systematic exposition of this geometric method. It contains some fifty geometrical diagrams with about 100 pages of descriptive text. It puts together into a single coherent account the modern geometrical analysis of the theory of international trade which at present can be studied only by consulting a large number of separate articles in different specialist journals. In addition, Professor Meade makes a number of original contributions, notably in the geometrical treatment of domestic production, of the balance of payments, and of import and export duties. It is probable that this work also will become a landmark in the development of its subject.

A NEO-CLASSICAL THEORY OF ECONOMIC GROWTH

'I should like to begin this review, rather unconventionally, by thanking Professor Meade for having written a book' (rather than a mere article). Thus Professor J. R. Hicks in his review in the *Economic Journal*, emphasizing the book's great importance in illuminating the interrelations of the various approaches to the theory of economic growth.

The second edition contained a good deal of new material, particularly a chapter on the case of unlimited supplies of labour and substantial alterations to the chapter on changes in the rate of economic growth.

This is the first paperback edition of Professor Meade's *Neo-Classical Theory*, which has itself become something of a classic.

J. E. MEADE

PLANNING AND THE PRICE MECHANISM

To plan or not to plan? This book outlines a solution of our present economic problems which makes the fullest use of the price mechanism and of free initiative and competition, but which involves the socialisation of certain monopolistic concerns and the state control of the price mechanism in such a way as to maintain full employment, to achieve an equitable distribution of income and property, and to restore equilibrium to our international balance of payments. It is an outline of that 'middle way' which the author calls the Liberal-Socialist solution.

The author is at present Professor of Commerce dealing with international economic problems at the University of London. He taught economics at Oxford from 1931 to 1937, and wrote the League of Nations' World Economic Surveys in Geneva from 1937 to 1940. During the war he was a member of the Economic Section of the Cabinet Secretariat and was Director of that Section for the first two years of post-war reconstruction, being a member of the United Kingdom delegations to various international conferences. In this book he has drawn on his wide domestic and international experience to apply his principles of Liberal-Socialism to a great range of current economic problems.

THE GROWING ECONOMY

In this sequel to *The Stationary Economy* Professor Meade continues his task as what he calls an up-to-date 'specialist in generalization'— the task of presenting a systematic treatment of the whole field of economic analysis in the form of a series of simplified models which are specially designed to show the interconnections between the various specialist fields of economic theory. While action always demands empirical enquiry, he is convinced from experience that the training in economic principles given by these models inculcates a way of looking at things which is invaluable in reaching sensible decisions. His work also offers students and specialists the boon of a general survey of the most sophisticated up-to-date theory in a form which demands a minimum of mathematical training. To quote *The Economist*, 'It is a long time since anyone attempted to write a treatise . . . on economic analysis in general. . . . This is a splendid and bold idea. Professor Meade is a master of lucid and rigorous theoretical exposition.'

MONEY AND FINANCE IN AFRICA

ERIN E. JUCKER-FLEETWOOD

This original study attempts to describe the problems faced and the solutions found by the monetary and financial authorities of six emerging African countries. Most of these countries have been visited, often repeatedly, by the author and her collaborators, who have had the privilege of first-hand information from the institutions concerned.

The special economic and even social factors of these African countries have been described and emphasis has been laid on the atmosphere of rapid change, growth and development. An attempt has been made to indicate the common denominators while making due allowance for the character of each individual country. The establishment of the Central Banks, the expansion of the system of commercial banks and other financial intermediaries has been described. The specific problems of monetary and financial policy in emerging countries has been discussed especially in relation to the financing of development plans and the balance of payments.

INFLATION AND THE THEORY OF MONEY

R. J. BALL

This book fills an important gap in the literature on macroeconomics with regard to the analysis of the determinants of the general price level, in an industrialised economy. The author restates conventional employment theory focusing attention on its implications for general price level analysis. The book goes on to survey contemporary literature on the determination of wages, prices and the demand for money, and to develop a framework within which to analyse the current problem of inflation.

GEORGE ALLEN AND UNWIN LTD

For Product Safety Concerns and Information please contact our EU
representative GPSR@taylorandfrancis.com Taylor & Francis Verlag GmbH,
Kaufingerstraße 24, 80331 München, Germany

Printed and bound by CPI Group (UK) Ltd, Croydon, CR0 4YY
08/05/2025
01864399-0002